VEGAN

AN INDIAN COOKBOOK

PERFECTION IN VEGAN INDIAN CUISINE. HANDCRAFTED FAMILY RECIPES STRAIGHT FROM THE HEART AND FROM AN AWARD-WINNING INDIAN RESTAURANT.

NIAZ CAAN

Grosvenor House
Publishing Limited

This book is published by
Grosvenor House Publishing Ltd
Link House
140 The Broadway, Tolworth, Surrey, KT6 7HT.
www.grosvenorhousepublishing.co.uk

A CIP record for this book
is available from the British Library

ISBN 978-1-80381-444-5

All recipes and this book have been created and authored by Niaz Caan.
Photography by Muhammad Baqir.

This book is dedicated to my family.
Because everything is for them,
and they make my life a harmony of happiness.

CONTENTS

INTRODUCTION

My first time making a curry…

It was a cold drizzly Tuesday afternoon after school. I was 13, hairy, breaking out, and a bit chubby. I had nothing better to do than be in the kitchen – an alien environment at a time when *The Simpsons* and video games were the highlight of my life. The 'sitting around doing nothing' got to my mum, and she had me shuffling my feet into the kitchen, for some stupid reason deciding to make me cook.

Telling me to pick up a spoon and start cooking, my mum walked me through how to make a Lamb Pathia.* A Pathia is a perfect balance of sweet, sour, and spice, and that one fateful evening had me hooked.

Mum talked me through it, yes, but wow! I was hooked. The smell of the toasted spices; the warm hue from the onions sweltering! I'd just started, but I was ready to replace my mum as the house cook. As I continued with my mum's direction, adding the lamb and the plethora of spices synonymous with Indian cooking, numerous questions circled around in my head. 'Am I cooking – like on TV? Can I leave school? Open a restaurant?'

As the dish gradually reduced, a beautiful tomato-red sauce greeted my eyes. I took a spoonful of this sauce, and OH MY GOD! A cacophony of the Pathia's sweet and sour tastes puzzled me with how my tongue was delighted yet conflicted. The combination of chilli powder and garam masala working perfectly with the succulent lamb made me realise that cooking is fantastic. However, I must admit that I had no part in cooking the lamb; that was down to Mum (love you, Mum).

Since then, I have been and am still constantly around food. I manage my award-winning restaurant in London, and when I'm not doing that, I am in the kitchen experimenting with new dishes that can wow my customers and me! And now I'm even writing about food!

It's the passion for food that's kept me experimenting, kept me cooking, kept me managing my restaurant and customers with love every day. So, when my new vegan menu for the restaurant began to attract rave reviews from customers, so many asked for the recipes that it felt only fitting for me to write a cookbook!

The way I describe food in this book might be unusual, and if you are over 40 and need help understanding some of the jokes or references, it might be best to ask a younger counterpart to explain. (Honestly, I've never tried hard so hard to write with 'good' English.)

I love food too much, but I've never compromised on taste. I remember buying a vegan cookbook once to find some ideas, only to find that it comprised 200 repurposed versions of cabbage on a plate… What the hell?

For all the customers who've asked me for the recipes – this book is for you. Or perhaps you've been given this book as a gift because you love everything vegan, or you love food and want to broaden your range of dishes. Whatever the reason, I hope you can use my book to create some amazing love in the kitchen; I'll have love for you for just trying!

These dishes are not relatively hard to cook – but they're vegan, they come from the heart, and they're new, soul-rivetingly flavourful, and wholesome.

I hope you enjoy this cookbook, from my restaurant kitchen in London to yours.

Love Niaz Caan x

My amazing and wonderful mother.

---

*I know it was bold of me to start a vegan cookbook talking about lamb, but please bear with me!

THANK YOU, CITY SPICE

THANK YOU FOR ALLOWING A SPACE FOR ME TO CREATE ONE OF THE BEST CURRY HOUSES IN LONDON, FOR THE BEST DINERS IN THE WORLD.

I might get emotional and serious here, but bear with me…

'Incredibly jubilant on a Monday evening. Buzzing with a mix of office workers and families. The cooking here is class, and it's no wonder this curry house is picking up awards by the Karahi-Load; the food is exquisite!' These were the words of one critic review for City Spice, and I certainly would agree.

City Spice has been home to my cooking and love since I was 17 years old. I started my culinary career when I was 14, somehow ending up in the kitchen of a takeaway in Kent. Like many young chefs starting out, mopping and cling film were the bane of my life.

However, over the next two years, I actively learned the ropes, picking up the masalas and cooking techniques and becoming such a good cook that I was running that takeaway full-time by the age of 16. I won't bore you with the details, but arduous would be one word to describe this career beginning.

However, when I was 17, I saw an opportunity to cook in London for a then run-down graffiti-torn restaurant in Brick Lane, called City Spice. I jumped on this ship because I believed in the vision we had for the restaurant. The aim? To turn this restaurant into one of the best places to eat Indian food in London over the next five years. How? Through inventive cooking, loving service, and bringing the bustling Indian atmosphere into the restaurant. We made the restaurant a beautifully unpretentious place to eat (bye-bye graffiti), made our service infallible, and began perfecting the menu to include well-loved favourites and new soon-to-be award-winning dishes.

Within 12 months, we had won two 'Best Indian Restaurant' awards and made the national newspapers. Over five years, we picked up several more awards, and now continuously crop up on TV for our cooking. We have also been mentioned in several more newspapers for the love we bring.

It was through City Spice that I learned true flavour mastery. Here, I learned the magical things that chefs can do: bringing people joy and happiness with food. Very few products in the world can spark an emotional reaction like food, and over the next few years, I learned how to harness this power.

I learnt from some of the most experienced chefs in the world about cooking curry, and I learnt about menu design and new recipes from Michelin-starred chefs. This led me to create my first menu, the acclaimed 'Michel-Indian Vegan Menu', at City Spice. And it sits alongside our award-winning 'Meat' menu, which has also received plaudits from critics and diners alike.

When I was 22, I became the executive chef at City Spice, being featured on Channel 5, Channel 4, online media, and newspapers, for my efforts.

I am fortunate to have a wonderfully supportive family, and lucky to have an excellent team continually pushing City Spice to more remarkable achievements.

I am also fortunate to have such loving diners from across the world to sample some of the love at City Spice. Through City Spice, I've met Scots, Australians, Chinese, Americans – all sorts of people! I am delighted they have chosen City Spice as their go-to restaurant when they visit London, and I am happy that we live up to their high expectations.

Now that I am the executive chef at City Spice, recipes, love, and dining have to elevate further. We must keep pushing this fantastic, beautifully restored eatery from strength to strength.

Honestly, without City Spice, I would not be in such a position and I would not be able to write this cookbook. So, thank you, City Spice. Thank you from the bottom of my heart. The love from the diners at City Spice and my family is why I want to continue progressing.

Anyway, tears over, back to being bubbly and not so serious. It's time to start cooking at home and having fun with the flavour in this book!

OUR KITCHEN NEEDS TO BE READY!

What our loaded cupboard needs so that we can cook like absolute flavour pros.

ALL-PURPOSE SEASONING:
The seasoning that did to food what colour TV did to the 1950s. This little cupboard secret needs to be in your cupboard till you like it so much that you display it on your mantelpiece. If there's only one spice mix in your spice rack – make sure it's this.

ROTIS:
Round, curvy, and voluptuous (*coughs* no, I'm describing food!), this wheat from India has fed us for 3000 years. Filling and healthy, this is a perfect companion to our vegan food. I've got the recipe for Rotis in here, but you can pre-cook and store these so that you're not sweating out in the kitchen making them daily.

CHICKPEAS:
A really good protein source for our vegan dishes. Roast and season them, and they can be incorporated into many 'saucy' dishes for some extra texture.

WHITE RICE (BROWN IS A BIT... DULL):
A stalwart side for almost every Indian dish. You'll need this, so make sure you know how to cook the rice! I've also included a few biriyani dishes to blow your mind, so make sure your rice skills are top-notch!

ONIONS:
Almost every dish in this book contains onions. If you are allergic to onions, well... that's a shame.

LEMON:
Squeeze them lemons! Lemons are a must-have to remove any harsh flavours in a dish, while you can also use the zest to be fancy (or if you're a stickler for instructions).

FRESH HERBS:
Coriander, mint, parsley, and thyme. As my brother says, 'Your dish needs to smell nice', and he's not wrong. Don't underestimate the power of these aromatic superheroes.

NAGA CHILLIES:
From the subcontinent, these chillies pack heat and may leave you in a heap of sweat and discomfort if you are faint-hearted. Still, at least the hint of sweetness helps. Give them a try, and if you are not a fan, swap them out for birds' eye chillies.

TOFU:
If it's not meat, we need to ensure it's neat. Tofu is the go-to substitute for vegan meat. The recipes in my book aren't just meat swap-outs but are specifically designed to bring out the best of tofu. Make sure tofu is always in your cupboard, ready to be cooked into vegan goodness.

MANGO JUICE:
An Indian man's water. Like Jesus gave wine to his disciples, God gave mango juice to the immigrants. Mango juice, paired with any vegan dish in this book, is a match made in heaven. Always serve stone cold, and for the milder dishes, opt for some fizzy mango juice.

MY BIGGEST RECOMMENDATION FOR EVERYTHING AND EVERYONE:

Now, like every other cookbook, I am giving you a pre-set ingredient list serving a number of BRITISH people (I say this because I have seen America's medium portions at their fast-food restaurants, and they are unbelievable).

I recommend certain spices for each dish, but I suggest you spice your dish to your liking, especially as you go on to cook more dishes from the book. Take some time, learn what each spice does to your palate – then make these dishes your own. Always salt and pepper to taste and use your judgment, i.e., if a curry dish is sticking to the pan, turn down the heat and add cold water!

 Look out for the City Spice stamp! These are dishes available all year round at my restaurant in Brick Lane, London!

Look out for golden coloured writing! These are tips from me to make your cooking even better!

PART ONE: STARTERS

STARTERS SO GOOD YOU'LL FORGET TO COOK THE MAINS!

CITY CHANA CHAT

Serves: **3-4 people**

Prep: **40 minutes**

Cook: **5 minutes**

INGREDIENTS

3 cups of canned chickpeas
(you can cook fresh chickpeas
instead; however, you need a
pressure cooker)

½ teaspoon salt
(or salt and pepper to taste)

1 medium-sized onion,
finely chopped

1 medium-sized tomato,
finely chopped

¼ of cucumber, finely chopped

1 green chilli, finely chopped

1 teaspoon cumin powder

1 teaspoon chilli powder

1 teaspoon chaat masala

½ teaspoon tamarind powder

½ a lemon to squeeze

Coriander to garnish

Tamarind sauce

This is an incredibly filling vegan starter that could make everyone at a dinner party wonder how the mains could be better. Chickpeas are cooked with spices and a refreshing tamarind sauce to produce a flavoursome and piquant dish. This recipe is a City Spice classic, so come down if you want it made for you!

INSTRUCTIONS

Preparation for Chana Chaat

First, we have to prep our ingredients, so make sure to rinse everything; don't be dirty! We start with the chickpeas, drain them from the water in the can, and then bring them to a boil in a pot covered with salted water, drain them (again), and set them to one side. Then, dice up the onions, tomato, cucumber, and chilli.

Put the chickpeas into a mixing bowl, add salt and pepper to taste, and then the following spices: chilli powder, cumin powder, tamarind powder, and mix! Also, add some chat masala and then mix again!

But even more mixing still needs to be done! Mix the chopped tomatoes, cucumber, diced onions, and chillies (although you can leave the chillies out if you do not like spice!). With all these new vegetables joining the party, get your hands into the bowl and mix well.

Once you have everything mixed, squeeze over the lemon juice and garnish with coriander. Serve it in a bowl with tamarind sauce drizzled all over, and enjoy the dish's beauty! Relatively easy!

ITTLE BITTLE SAMOSAS

Serves: **3-4 people**
(Makes around 25 in total)

Prep: **50 minutes**

Cook: **15-20 minutes inclusive**

INGREDIENTS

1 pastry sheet

3 medium potatoes

1 carrot

½ medium onion, finely diced

1.5L of oil for frying
(sunflower oil is perfect)

½ teaspoon turmeric powder

Salt and pepper to taste

1 teaspoon chilli powder

1 teaspoon paprika

2 teaspoons all-purpose seasoning

¼ teaspoon garam masala

¼ teaspoon cumin powder

An adorable family starter recipe taught to me by my mum and stuffed with a filling that is second to none. This starter has a lot of steps and may be a little trickier than some others, but the flavour and impact these have in your mouth is so worth it!

INSTRUCTIONS

First, we must prepare the actual samosas, which includes prepping our sweet vegetable mix to be stuffed inside them! Firstly, boil the potatoes in a saucepan (with salted water) to soften them and nicely cook them out. Then drain and skin the potatoes before mashing them in a mixing bowl. Once the potatoes are mashed, set them aside and prepare to start on the carrot. Carrots give the samosa a beautiful crunch and bring out the sweetness of the filling.

Get a saucepan, and fill it with salted water, then take a carrot, peel it, chop it into tiny cube pieces, and boil. Once cooked, take it out, and that's the carrot done!

Now we need to add flavour to our filling! Take a small pan and heat some oil. Add chopped onion, ginger, garlic, and sauté until translucent (this is your onion base).

Now, add the spices listed in the ingredients list (add all of them) into your onion base. Then add the mashed potatoes and the carrot to your onion base, and mix everything. Take a step back and admire your skills as a chef before adding salt to your taste, and tasting your mix to confirm that you are an outstanding chef.

Continued on page 6…

1 teaspoon coriander powder

---

1 teaspoon ginger + garlic minced/finely chopped

Fresh chives, finely chopped for garnish

Fresh coriander, finely chopped

A squeeze of a lemon

Vegan mint sauce and mango/green chutney

Finally, add the juice of a fresh lemon and garnish with a small amount of chopped coriander. Let the mixture go cold as you move onto the pastry. (Don't worry, these get fried, so it's not a cold starter!)

Now, onto the pastry and filling them in (the tricky part)! Dust your surface with some flour and place the pastry sheet on the surface. With a rolling pin, spread the sheet out so that it is all nice, even, and flat. After doing this, brush the sheet with oil before carefully rolling the sheet from one side to the other into a flat triangle shape. Brush this with oil, and then fold again to have a smaller triangle. Fold lengthways across, brush with oil, and fold again. If you lift this from your surface, you will have a small cone to stuff your heavenly potato-carrot mix in!

Use the excess of the pastry shape to close off the now pyramid shape and set it aside. Brush with some oil and repeat until you have enough Samosas.

Now that the 'ittle bittles' are all stuffed and ready to be cooked, you have to fry them! Get a deep pan with hot oil, heat to frying temperature (180°C), and fry them until they are golden brown and crispy! Ensure not to clutter the pan when cooking, and fry for approximately 6-8 minutes.

Once cooked, set them aside on some kitchen towel to drain the excess oil, garnish with some chopped chives, then leave to cool before enjoying them! They go great with some condiments such as mango chutney and mint sauce!

TIP: You can make your puff pastry if you can, or buy it if pressed for time. Whatever you do, make sure the puff pastry is tight enough so you can bop it, twist it, and pull it)

ITTLE BITTLE SAMOSAS

SAMMY'S KEBABS

SAMMY'S KEBABS

INGREDIENTS

1 chopped potato

1 glug of olive oil

1 cup chopped cauliflower florets

1 medium carrot

6-7 button mushrooms

1 medium onion

¼ cup green peas, fresh or frozen

10 fresh mint leaves

2 tablespoons chopped coriander leaves

1 teaspoon ginger-garlic paste

10 tablespoons of gram flour

Salt and pepper to taste

1 teaspoon turmeric powder

1 teaspoon red chilli powder

I used to work front of house in an Indian eatery when I was about 14. It was my first job, and I had to answer the phones, serve customers, and pack takeaway bags. Over time, I ended up managing the establishment. However, one particular day, an Indian bloke came into the takeaway, asking for a 'Sammy kebab' starter in a distinct Indian accent. I did not know who Sammy even was, let alone that he had made a kebab, but people being people... he thought if he said it louder, and louder, and louder, I would somehow understand what he meant. I understood nothing and could've burst into tears, thinking that I would get fired. Eventually, it transpired that the bloke wanted a 'Shami Kebab' (a flat version of an Indian meat kebab). At 14, I hated that day! So, aggressive Indian man, this self-invented vegan dish is for you.

INSTRUCTIONS

First, we will take the vegetables (which I hope you washed before cutting!) and put them in a blender. Along with the vegetables, add in some mint and coriander for aroma and blend the vegetables. Keep blending until the veggies mince, but be careful of mincing too much or the vegetables become a smoothie – and we don't want that!

Transfer this mince into a mixing bowl, season to your taste with the above dry spices, and salt and pepper the mince. Mix in some oil and ginger-garlic paste, then get your elbows in (not literally; your hands will do) and mix well.

Preheat your oven to 180°C – we'll need it later.

Continued on page 10...

1 teaspoon garam masala

Fresh chives, finely chopped, for garnish

Get a pan over some low heat and add the gram flour. This part can be a bit tricky; keep toasting the flour away until it toasts, and you can see a slight colour change, at which point add this roasted gram flour to the mixture you have made! Check if the combination is to taste and mix well (again).

Now, here's the fun bit! Grab a portion of the veggie mince and roll it into a flat patty that fits the palm of your hand – use those Play-Doh skills! Repeat this with all the mince until you have many patties, then take a baking tray greased with olive oil, line it with some parchment paper, and align all these balls on your tray! Transfer to the oven and let them bake for 20-25 minutes.

While the kebabs are baking, maybe ponder the fact that it is claimed more people now speak English with an Indian accent than people with a British accent (the Queen's English)! So perhaps these *should* be called Sammy's kebabs?

Take the patties out after 10-15 minutes, and look: beautiful! Plate them and serve them with a good portion of mango chutney and vegan mint sauce. Garnish with chives.

ALOO CHAT

INGREDIENTS

4 potatoes, peeled, boiled, and cubed

1 onion, finely chopped

1 handful of fresh coriander, chopped

1 green chilli, finely chopped

Green chutney

Mango chutney

1 teaspoon cumin powder

1 teaspoon coriander powder

1 teaspoon chilli powder

2 teaspoons all-purpose seasoning

1 fresh lemon for squeezing

Finely chopped spring onions for garnish

1-2 tablespoons oil

Salt and pepper to taste

Go to a street café in Mumbai and talk about having starters; it's usually this dish. A simple starter, the effort-to-taste ratio means that it's an easy dish, but it tastes so good that you could lie to all your friends about how many hours it took to cook, and they'd believe you! A piquant blend of potatoes and chat masala, while topped with pomegranate seeds and mango chutney (optional) so that it tastes even better. Aloo Chat is one of my favourite vegan starters.

INSTRUCTIONS

Luckily, chaat does not need a lot of steps. Wash, then boil your potatoes before dicing them into small-sized chunks. Throw these into a pan that's already hot with oil, then shallow-fry these chunks until they are golden brown! Take them out once golden brown and leave to dry a bit on some kitchen paper.

Now, in a bowl, add the potatoes and the following: salt (to taste), cumin powder, coriander powder, chilli powder, all-purpose seasoning, chillies, and a squeeze of lemon. Then get your hands in and mix it well! Once that's done, you can serve it in a bowl and garnish with some spring onions!

POTATO PEPPER POPPERS

Serves: **3-4 people**
(Makes 4 poppers)

Prep: **25 minutes**

Cook: **15 minutes**

INGREDIENTS

3 medium-sized potatoes

1 carrot

2 handfuls of garden peas

4 bell peppers

1 onion

2 teaspoons cumin powder

3 cloves chopped garlic

1 teaspoon red chilli powder

2 teaspoons garam masala

2 teaspoons all-purpose seasoning

2 teaspoons dried fenugreek seeds

Salt and pepper to taste

Coriander, chopped

Okay, this is one to use when you need to impress your other half (as if the other dishes didn't). Please take what you know about Indian food appetisers and unite it into a succulent bell pepper that falls apart at the fork. And as the pepper is the star of the show here, we might as well keep it intact in its beautiful form.

INSTRUCTIONS

Boil the potatoes (peel these first), the carrot, and the peas. But do not boil the pepper (or onions)! Dice the onion finely and chop the ginger.

Wash out the pepper and delicately slice just the top off, then use a spoon and knife to empty the bell pepper so that you're left with an open-top shell that you can stuff.

Now onto the stuffing. Heat a pan with oil on medium heat, drop in the diced onions and chopped ginger, and let them cook for two minutes. Add cumin powder, fenugreek seeds, chilli powder, garam masala, and all-purpose seasoning. Let this sauté, and mix until the onions are golden brown but coloured from the seasoning! Once cooked, add in your boiled vegetables, using a wooden spoon (or something that won't scratch your pan!) to mash the vegetables while they are cooking. Mix well with the spices and admire your stuffing!

Next, gently stuff the poppers (as I call them) with the stuffing, then place them back in the pan upright and cover the pan to let them cook for 12 minutes (this ensures that they are crunchy and grilled correctly). Once that's done, crack salt and pepper over the finished dish and serve.

TIP: When putting the poppers in the oven, if you have a vegan cheese that you like, sprinkle it all over the peppers to add some thickness and bring out some more flavour in the starter!

TOFU TIKKA SKEWERS (OOOFT!)

Serves: **4 people**
(Makes 4 skewers)

Prep: **10 minutes**

Cook: **20 minutes**

INGREDIENTS

16 oz block tofu cut into
1-inch cubes

1 large red onion, thickly sliced

2 bell peppers (1 red and
1 green) cut into 1-inch pieces

2 tablespoons red chilli powder

2 teaspoons garam masala

3 teaspoons all-purpose
seasoning

2 teaspoons curry powder

1 teaspoon of mixed
herbs powder

2 garlic cloves, finely minced

½ inch ginger, finely minced

A squeeze of half a lemon

½ cup vegan yogurt
(choose your favourite brand)

Salt and pepper to taste

Oil of your choice
(but not coconut!)

Mango chutney

Vegan mint sauce

Let me transform what you know about vegan and Indian food with this starter. It's so simple to cook, yet so succulent, as you're letting the grill do all the work. In this section, this is my favourite, cooked up and perfected in the City Spice kitchen at 3am. A meatless beauty, tofu is terrific for being a quality source of protein. Yet, being such a versatile product, it means when making these skewers, you can effortlessly cook them to perfection.

INSTRUCTIONS

Get a large mixing bowl for your marinade and whack it on the table for extra effect. In the bowl, add your cubed tofu, yogurt, chilli powder, garam masala, curry powder, all-purpose seasoning, ginger, mixed herbs, garlic, a squeeze of lemon juice, and salt. Optionally, you can add some red dye here if you'd like your tofu to look colourful! Mix well and let them all get to know each other.

After they've become friends, add the bell peppers and thickly sliced onions to the mix, then let it sit in the fridge for 30 minutes at least (2 hours is better; overnight is the best!).

Now, getting a skewer, assemble this however you like. I usually put the vegetables, tofu, then vegetables again, tofu again, then vegetables to finish. Once that's done, you're ready to cook the skewers of tofu and veg. You can cook them on an open pan with oil heated on medium, rotating until all sides are well done (should take about 20 mins in total).

Alternatively, the oven is also a great way to get them grilled; stick the skewers over a baking tray, grill them at 200°C, rotating them as each side gets grilled (each side should take around 5-8 minutes).

Serve in a bowl, and drizzle mango chutney and mint sauce over them if you like to get messy. Then enjoy!

BHINDI BANGERS

Serves: **3 people**

Prep: **15 minutes**

Cook: **15 minutes**

INGREDIENTS

½ teaspoon chaat masala

3 tablespoons chickpea flour

2 teaspoons chilli powder

1 teaspoon ground turmeric

2 teaspoons ground coriander

½ teaspoon ground cumin

Salt and pepper to taste

Sunflower oil for deep-frying

600g okra, topped, tailed, cut in half lengthways, and left to dry on kitchen paper for 30 minutes (excess moisture can lead to soggy bangers!)

Take some okra, and slice it so it's tall and slender, like a supermodel. Season each slice so they have some oomph when they meet your mouth, then fry them! That's the simplicity of these Bhindi Bangers, yet the result is so moreish that, just like chips, you can never have enough of them! A perfect starter recipe – crisp and cool!

INSTRUCTIONS

Grab a bowl and mix your dry spices, the chat masala, and chickpea flour. Fellow cooks, this is the perfect match for your okra, which has the flavour once spiced. Add salt and pepper to your taste then add some water so the flour and spice mix becomes a paste.

Place the okra into your bowl with the paste and rub the okra in, ensuring the slices are well coated.

Get a deep enough pan for frying and pour in the amount of oil you need (about 1/3 of your pan) to fry your okra. Heat the pan over medium-high heat ensuring that when you drop okra in, the oil should sizzle! Fry your okra in batches for about 7 minutes per batch!

Once fried, set your okra to the side on some kitchen paper and pat the oil off, so that each slice is dry and crispy. Sprinkle over your spice mixture, and salt and pepper your okra well. Serve in a bowl with some mint sauce and mango chutney!

Tip: Try and keep the okra as dry as possible. Pat them with a paper towel if you need to, as this removes excess moisture, maximising the crispiness!

PALANI POTATO LOLLIPOP BALLS

Serves: **30 balls,
enough for two people**

Prep: **30 minutes**

Cook: **10 minutes**

INGREDIENTS

4 medium potatoes, boiled and drained (I'd recommend Russet potatoes or Maris Pipers, as they have a lovely creamy texture due to their starch)

1.5L of oil for frying (sunflower oil is perfect)

1 onion, diced finely

Chopped chives, for garnish

1 teaspoon of chaat masala, also for garnish

½ cup of breadcrumbs

1 teaspoon of garlic-ginger paste

1 teaspoon of garlic powder

1 teaspoon of chilli powder

Salt and pepper to taste

1 teaspoon of red chilli flakes

Continued on page 20…

A starter recipe that doesn't make sense why it tastes so good yet it's so simple to make. Crunchy on the outside but flavourful, with a lovely texture inside. These cute little potato balls beat meatballs 1-0.

INSTRUCTIONS

Mash the cooked potatoes into a mixing bowl, then add in the diced onions, the ginger-garlic paste, the chives, and the following seasoning: all-purpose, chilli, thyme, oregano, garlic, chives, and salt and pepper to taste. Get your hands in and start mixing!

Once everything is mixed and you're happy with the seasoning taste (if you are a beginner, don't worry; it will turn out amazing), stick the bowl in the fridge and let the mixture set. Half an hour should do it; overnight is better.

Lightly grease your hands with a little oil, then take the mixture and make approximately 25-35 balls, each one taking up about a quarter of your palm. Either roll the balls on a flat surface or in your hand (like Play-Doh!)

Now we need to make the wet batter. This wet paste will let the breadcrumbs stick to the potato balls to give them a crispy texture. Make the paste by mixing corn starch into the water; once the batter is consistent enough for coating, you can set it aside.

Then, take your breadcrumbs, season with chilli flakes, oregano, and thyme, and set aside.

2 teaspoons of all-purpose seasoning

_____

½ lemon (for squeezing)

_____

1 teaspoon of thyme

_____

1 teaspoon of oregano

_____

3 tablespoons of corn starch

_____

Mint sauce (vegan) and mango chutney

_____

Now, take your potato balls, dip them into the wet batter and then into the breadcrumbs mix, making sure each ball is covered well with breadcrumbs! Do this for all the balls.

Now that everything is ready, get your oil hot and ready for frying. Dip the balls in and cook until the balls are crispy, golden, and glowing like your beautiful self.

Once cooked, take the balls out and set them aside on some paper towels to allow the excess oil to be patted out.

Garnish the balls with some chives and chaat masala, then drizzle mango chutney and mint sauce all over them for saucy goodness.

N.B. Chaat masala you can find at many Asian corner shops! They're like magic powder, used to amplify the flavour of dry dishes.

Tip: Take off the crust and use white bread when making the breadcrumbs! This keeps the balls crispier and ensures they absorb less grease!

PALANI POTATO LOLLIPOP BALLS

SWEETIE-MADE TOFU

Serves: **4 people**

Prep: **40 minutes**

Cook: **25 minutes**

INGREDIENTS

For the tikka paste:

2 tablespoons coconut oil, melted

2 cloves garlic, minced

2 teaspoons fresh ginger, finely diced

2 teaspoons brown sugar

2 hot chillies, finely chopped (Bird's Eye are fab)

2 tablespoons tomato puree

2 tablespoons garam masala

1 tablespoon cumin

1 tablespoon coriander

1 tablespoon paprika

1 teaspoon turmeric

½ teaspoon salt

¼ teaspoon fenugreek

½ teaspoon lime juice

Continued on page 24…

Take the tikka masala, stick a skewer through it, and grill it. Then on this skewer is a delectable, sweet with a hint of spice, juicy piece of tofu. Served over a bed of lightly seasoned sweet potato, I promise this is a starter bursting with flavour, and a privilege to eat. Filling and healthy, you can double up the portions and serve it with rice as a healthy dinner, too! But being a glutton, I'm going to leave this as a starter. Yesssss…

INSTRUCTIONS

Sweetie-made tofu is essentially a sweet version of the tofu skewers we showed you earlier, but I promise this dish bursts with the flavour you deserve! We're going to start by making our tofu tikka marinade, so take all of the ingredients listed in the 'tikka paste' section and blend them all in a blender to make a nice delicate marinade – this is the sweet, sweet, sweet marinade for the tofu!

Grab your tofu and place it in a mixing bowl, drop some olive oil into the bowl, and pour in your marinade. Mix well!

Then let this sit in the fridge for at least 30 minutes. Overnight is best, if possible –we need the masala flavour from the marinade to get to know the tofu, so they mix well!

Now turn your oven on, preheating it to 180°C.

Next, line out your sweet potato in a baking tray and pour in some olive oil. Season well with salt, pepper, and brown sugar. Toss the potato around in the baking tray to mix everything well.

For the curry:

1 tablespoon olive oil

600g sweet potato,
peeled and cubed

---

3 medium-sized onions,
cut into half-moons

---

2 teaspoons brown sugar

Then, take the tofu tikka covered in the beautiful marinade, and skewer them, oscillating between tofu and onion. Then layer the skewers over the potatoes on the baking tray. As the tofu cooks, if any marinade drops, the sweet potatoes can capture that flavour for an extreme burst of taste!

Let the entire dish cook in the oven for 20-25 minutes, then take it out of the oven for cooling for 10 minutes before garnishing with coriander.

Serve this delectable dish with some vegan mint sauce and mango chutney! Yummy!

SO GOOD, SO POPULAR, ONION BHAJIS

Serves: **4 people**

Prep: **30 minutes**

Cook: **10 minutes**

INGREDIENTS

2 large red onions, thinly sliced

1 cup gram flour/
chickpea flour

1 teaspoon cumin powder

1 teaspoon coriander powder

½ teaspoon ground turmeric

½ teaspoon chilli powder

¼ cup coriander leaves

Salt and pepper to taste

1-3 teaspoons water, as needed

Chives, chopped for garnish

Visit a café in Delhi (not Starbucks; why would you?), and onion bhajis seems to be the most popular starter item there. Come 6000 miles to a little island called Britain, and onion bhajis seem to be even more popular. Onion bhajis are universally loved, so it is only right we perfect them, add a little twist, make sure they're vegan, and bring some love into the kitchen through them.

INSTRUCTIONS

Okay, let's grab a mixing bowl and add the onions, flour, all the powdered spices, and some salt to your taste. Get your hands in, mix incredibly well, and then let this onion mixture sit for about an hour at room temperature. After an hour, squeeze out any excess moisture from the onions and mix into a batter. If you need moisture, add water one teaspoonful at a time!

Get some vegetable oil ready for frying. Take a saucepan and fill it about ⅓ full of oil, make sure the oil is very hot (approximately 180°C), and then add small amounts of batter at a time to fry. The onions should sizzle, and that's how you know the oil is hot enough!

Fry these onion batters for about 5-6 minutes a batch (do not overcrowd your saucepan, otherwise you will burn yourself because oil spits and kicks!). Once the onions are brown all over, you have fried them to perfection! Take them out, leave them on a paper towel, and pat dry to remove the excess moisture!

Please take a minute to admire the beautiful bhajis you've made while they cool. Garnish with chives and serve these established favourites with some mango chutney!

Tip: Avoid making the bhajis too big, or they can fall apart when frying. Smaller bhajis are also far easier to keep crispy!

PART TWO: MAIN COURSES

CURRIES

MAINS THAT CAN CURRY FLAVOUR WITH ABSOLUTELY ANYONE

PALANI POTATOES

INGREDIENTS

2 tablespoons oil

1½ teaspoons turmeric powder

2 teaspoons all-purpose seasoning

8 ozs of vegan curry base (see page 117)

1 teaspoon curry powder

1 heaped teaspoon of cumin seeds

10-15 fresh green curry leaves

Freshly chopped coriander (to garnish and also for cooking)

5 cloves of crushed garlic

4 green chillies, chopped finely

1½ inch ginger, crushed

5 red potatoes, diced into small cubes

Salt and pepper to taste

Spring onion, for garnish

Lemon juice from half a lemon

You make a beautiful sauce, some beautifully crisp potatoes to go with that it, and spiced to make sure they look good together. Then you drop in some cumin seeds and curry leaves to add some zestiness to the relationship, and BAM! – it's a match made in heaven. Palani Potatoes are a personal favourite of mine.

INSTRUCTIONS

Let's start by getting a pan out over medium heat and adding some oil. Once the oil is hot, we want to make the kitchen smell nice, so add the cumin seeds and curry leaves to toast these ingredients while enjoying the aroma. Once the cumin seeds pop, add some chopped coriander, garlic, chilli, and ginger. Make sure the garlic doesn't burn and stick to the pan! You can deal with this by turning down the heat and continuously stirring (hard work on the elbows).

Once the garlic starts to brown, let's add the real stuff. Add the potatoes and season them in the pan with all-purpose seasoning, curry powder, turmeric powder, and salt to your taste. Make sure everything is stirred nicely and mixed. If you need to add anything – do. From here, add your remarkable vegan curry base, which is the sauce base for this dish! Then put the lid on the pan and let the potatoes cook (should take no more than 10 minutes).

Once cooked, lay it out beautifully on a plate, serve with rice, and garnish with coriander for more fragrance.

VEGAN TOFU TIKKA MASALA MASALA

Serves: **3-4 people**

Prep: **70 minutes**

Cook: **40 minutes**

INGREDIENTS

For the Tofu and Marinade:

1 (14-ounce) package of tofu, firm or extra firm, well pressed

4 ounces soy yogurt

1 tablespoon sunflower oil

1 tablespoon lemon juice

1 teaspoon turmeric

1 teaspoon garam masala

1 teaspoon chilli powder

2 teaspoons paprika

2 teaspoons of all-purpose seasoning

2 teaspoons curry powder

1 teaspoon cumin powder

Salt and pepper to taste

This vegan dish is so good it's going to have you singing masala masala twice, like the Minions! A genuine no bulls**t vegan alternative to the Chicken Tikka Masala in Britain, this dish shows a new beginning. An excellent thick sauce with beautifully flavoursome chunks of tofu, this is a salivating, protein-rich curry dish that is so moreish it will have you longing for seconds.

INSTRUCTIONS

Let's begin straight away with the star of the show, the tofu! Start by cutting the pressed tofu into bite-sized cubes and arranging them into a bowl. The cuts should be about an inch cube in thickness. Add some olive oil and the yogurt.

Then, add all the spices that have been listed for the tofu and get to mixing! It's a flavour-rich curry, so there's a lot of seasoning, but it's got the reasoning! Squeeze the juice of one lemon into the bowl. Following this, wrap the bowl with Clingfilm and stick this marinade in the fridge for at least 30 minutes. However, as usual, overnight is best!

Once marinated, we can cook the tofu chunks, and the best way is to bake them in the oven. It'll take around 40 minutes, at a setting of 200°C, and slowly rotate them as they cook through!

Continued on page 32…

For the vegan Tikka Masala:

1 tablespoon olive oil or other neutral oil, such as canola or sunflower

---

1 can of crushed tomatoes, undrained

½ teaspoon ground cumin

---

1 teaspoon turmeric

---

1 teaspoon garam masala

---

1 teaspoon chilli powder

---

2 teaspoons paprika

---

2 teaspoons of all-purpose seasoning

---

4 ounces of soy yogurt

Chopped coriander, for garnish

Chopped spring onion, for garnish

As your protein is cooking, we can prepare the sauce. Get a pan with olive oil over medium heat. Add the tomatoes, spices mentioned, and soy yogurt, to bring out a beautiful reddish-orange dish. Once the sauce is well mixed and bubbling slightly, add in the tofu. Serve this wonderful British dish with some white rice, garnish with coriander and spring onions, and mop it up with a Roti, too!

Tip: Not exactly a tip, but it's essential, like the Covid vaccines. Make sure your tofu is extra firm! Anything else falls apart when cooking, and the next thing you know you have a dreary sludge of tasteless tofu that ruins your dish and reminds you of lockdown.

VEGAN TOFU TIKKA MASALA MASALA

CHOWLE ACHAR

CHOWLE ACHAR

Serves: **3-4 people**

Prep: **30 minutes**

Cook: **15-20 minutes**

INGREDIENTS

1½ cups water

1 teaspoon turmeric

1 teaspoon chilli powder

1 teaspoon garam masala

1 teaspoon curry powder

2 teaspoons all-purpose seasoning

1 teaspoon cumin powder

A pinch of salt, plus more to taste

9ozs of vegan curry base

1 can of chickpeas

1 tablespoon tamarind paste

2 tablespoons cumin seeds

1½ tablespoons of garlic-ginger paste

Continued on page 36…

A City Spice star, this one was a staff curry attempt at Veganuary, made with a City Spice twist. We get some beautiful Kabuli chickpeas sautéed quickly in some dry spices, then we blend this with some lovely pickle for a hint of sourness. If you want to try something new in Indian cuisine, this would be a tasty place to start.

INSTRUCTIONS

Right, first, we are going to prep our spice mix. A beautiful blend of Indian spices, it's good to make this first and have your flavour ready to go. On a plate, place all the powdered spices you need, except the cumin seeds, then mix them. Leave the cumin seeds to use when you're cooking.

In a separate saucepan, bring ½ cup of water to the boil, drain the chickpeas from the can, and drop these drained beauties into the saucepan. Season the water with a bit of salt, and cook for about 25 minutes.

In the meantime, get another pan over medium heat and add your oil; as it simmers, drop in your chopped onions, and let them brown. As the onions turn translucent, add your garlic-ginger paste and stir it in! Now drop in the spice mix! Let this mix in the pan till the onions colour due to the spices (the smell should be AMAZING!), and then add your vegan curry base. Add about 3ozs (Google this if you're not sure how much it is).

2 teaspoons of lime pickle

———————————————

1 tablespoon oil

———————————————

3 bay leaves

———————————————

1 small onion, chopped

———————————————

2 teaspoons garam masala

———————————————

1 lemon, squeezed

———————————————

Chopped coriander to garnish

———————————————

Let this simmer, then add another 6ozs of the vegan curry base. The vegan curry base is essentially your sauce, all flavoured and perfect (you can see the recipe for the vegan curry base on page 117). But we need to make this dish the ideal Chowle Achar that it is, so we add some tamarind sauce, the pickle, and the cumin seeds to the curry, and then turn the heat down to low. Let the curry come to a simmer, add your cooked chickpeas, squeeze the juice of an entire lemon over the dish, and then garnish with coriander!

SHOBJI KUFTA BHUJON

Serves: **3-4 people**

Prep: **60 minutes**

Cook: **15-20 minutes**

INGREDIENTS

N.B. All the seasonings mentioned below apply twice, so create two spice powders, one to marinate your SKB balls (yum) and the other to flavour the dish when you are cooking! (i.e., 1 teaspoon of turmeric is for the SKB ball, and then another 1 teaspoon for the curry).

1½ cups water

1 cup of canola oil

1 teaspoon turmeric

1 teaspoon chilli powder

1 teaspoon garam masala

1 teaspoon curry powder

1 teaspoon paprika

1 teaspoon mixed herb seasoning

2 teaspoons all-purpose seasoning

1 teaspoon cumin powder

A pinch of salt plus more to taste

9ozs of vegan curry base (see page 117)

Continued on page 38…

I love this dish so much. My favourite dish at City Spice, it is a bonanza of vegetables – including mushrooms, tomatoes, and peppers – in a thick sauce that is so delightful I could eat it all the time! Partially responsible for my 'big-boned' body when I was younger, this dish is so mouth-watering, so moreish, that I actually do eat it all the time…

INSTRUCTIONS

This dish can be tricky, so take a deep breath, try and pay extra attention to this recipe, and when you kill this dish in the kitchen and it tastes ABSOLUTELY AWESOME, know that you are a certified cook, and people should worship you…

We'll start by making the SKB balls, which are crucial to making this dish unique. Get a saucepan filled with boiling salted water and cook the following vegetables. You can boil the cauliflower florets and beans together, then do the potatoes (only 400g please), the carrots, and the peas.

You could boil them all together (apart from the potatoes) if you'd like, as the next step means the raw texture of the vegetables aren't necessary. Place all these vegetables into a plastic bowl, get a potato masher, and… mash! That's right, mash all the vegetables together until you can't recognise them.

Season this mash with all the powdered spices listed above and salt to your taste. Now the next step is to grab a handful of this mash and gently roll it into a ball – hence an SKB ball! Once you have rolled all the balls, bring out a deep pan filled with canola oil, ready for frying, and fry these balls one at a time for about three minutes until the colour of the balls changes to a brownish colour! Set all these aside, and pat dry where possible with some kitchen paper. Let them cool… without eating them.

3 teaspoons of tomato puree

2 tablespoons methi (fenugreek seeds)

1½ tablespoons of garlic-ginger paste

500 grams of baby potatoes (all without skin: 400 grams whole, and then separate 100g and chop these into small chunks)

1 can of cannellini beans

250g of carrots

250g of cauliflower florets

200g of garden peas

1 teaspoon of tomato paste

100g of cherry tomatoes

200g of mushrooms (I would recommend Portobellos due to their creaminess compared to other mushrooms)

1 tablespoon oil

3 bay leaves

2 cloves

4 green cardamom

3 curry leaves

1 small onion, chopped

1 lemon, squeezed

Chopped coriander to garnish

After the balls, the curry is next!

Put a pan over medium heat and toast the dry spices such as the bay leaves, cloves, and cardamom seeds; as this simmers, drop in your chopped onions and let them brown. Then add your garlic-ginger paste and stir it into your onions before adding the powdered spices (all over again from the ingredients list) and mix well. The onions should have changed colour because of the spices! Then drop in 3ozs of your vegan curry base! (You can see the recipe for the base on page 117!)

Let the dish simmer, and add your mushrooms, the chopped 100g of potatoes, the tomato puree, and the curry leaves! Add the rest of your vegan curry base (6ozs) before dropping in your SKB balls!

Stir gently, squeeze a lemon over the dish, garnish with coriander, and serve! Then pat yourself on the back for making such a masterpiece! You could also roast a sweet pepper and tomato to use in the dish!

Tip: Frying the SKB balls can be tricky, so use tongs and dip each ball into the oil slowly. Once the entire ball is submerged and is cooking, only then release the tongs from the ball and let it fry!

SHOBJI KUFTA BHUJON

COULD MURDER A DAAL MASALDER

COULD MURDER A DAAL MASALDER

INGREDIENTS

2½ cups, toor dal

2½ cups, channa dal

½ cup, moong dal

2 tomatoes, chopped

4 green chillies, slit

2 teaspoons chilli powder

2½ teaspoons turmeric powder

2 teaspoons coriander powder

2½ teaspoons cumin powder

A squeeze of half a lemon

2 tablespoons oil

4 cloves

If you want to make a superb, simple, and filling dish, the Daal Masalder is your go-to. A combination of exotic-sounding lentils with a good number of aromatic spices makes this a jack-of-all-trades for main courses. Healthy, flavoursome, and incredibly filling! When shopping, head to the world foods aisle and study carefully, as this dish uses three types of lentils!

INSTRUCTIONS

Okay, we first need to get all these lentils mingling, so wash all the lentils together and then add with 2 cups of water into a pot. Then add the turmeric powder and chillies, and let the water boil (we need to get those lentils cooking!). Once the water reaches boiling temperature, cover the pot with a lid and let the lentils simmer for about 20 minutes until they cook – once cooked, drain these and you should have beautiful, luscious yellow lentils. That's the daal part, now onto the masalder!

Leaving the lentils aside, bring out a pan and drop the oil in, then let that warm over medium heat. Once hot enough, drop in the dry spices to give some aroma to the dish. The dry spices are cloves, cardamoms, and ginger-garlic paste. Let the spices toast before adding the onions to sauté. Once the onions caramelise into a nice golden-brown colour and reduce in size, you have an excellent base. Add the tomatoes (salt them just as you put them into the pan) and let them cook with the onions. Once

Continued on page 42…

3 cardamoms

---

2 finely chopped onions

---

2 teaspoons ginger-garlic paste

---

2 tablespoons coriander leaves, chopped

Salt and pepper to taste

½ red onion, sliced for garnish

---

cooked, drop the cooked lentils into the base (mash these lentils if you want), and then add the powdered spices and salt to your taste!

Let everything get to know each other and leave to simmer for about 4 minutes. After a minute, drop in the slit chillies and let these cook a bit. Once all mixed in, garnish with coriander and sliced red onions, then serve with rice and roti!

DAAL BEGUN GATTA

INGREDIENTS

½ cup dried brown lentils

2 cups water

¼ cup olive oil

1 medium aubergine, cut into ½ inch cubes

1 onion, diced

3 garlic cloves, minced

2 green chillies, slit

1 teaspoon freshly grated ginger

2 teaspoons garam masala to taste

1 teaspoon chilli powder

2 teaspoons of curry powder

1 teaspoon ground cumin

1 14oz can of crushed tomatoes

Daal Begun Gatta has been a staple classic in my restaurant long before I was good enough to be in the kitchen. Daal Begun Gatta is a fan-favourite amongst diners, so it was essential to include it in this recipe book. A stunning dish, lentils and aubergine are carefully simmered and spiced to bring as much flavour out of the vegetables as possible. The vegetables then merge into a sauce fit for kings. A medium-spiced dish, the thick sauce, aubergine, and lentil mixture is tantalisingly delicious.

INSTRUCTIONS

Place the lentils into a small saucepan and cover them with 2 cups of water. We'll cook them first, so bring this water to a boil and then cover them with a lid for about 30 minutes. Once cooked, drain the lentils and set these aside. Mhhhhmmm, stare at them for a minute because they look so lovely!

While the lentils are cooking, you can get on with the rest of the dish! Get a pan over medium heat and drop in a glug of olive oil, garlic, bay leaves, cloves, and garlic-ginger paste. Once the oil is hot, add in one of the show's stars – the aubergine (or eggplant for you 'Muricans) – and the onions. Let these vegetables cook for about 7 minutes so the aubergine can soften while the onions become translucent. After this, we can add our powdered spices, salt, and pepper.

Continued on page 44…

1 14oz can of diced tomatoes

Salt and pepper to taste

---

2 teaspoons garlic-ginger paste

---

2 bay leaves

---

3 cloves

¼ cup chopped fresh coriander

Then get your chopped tomatoes, salt them lightly, and add to the pan. Let all this simmer until the aubergine is very tender (may take 10-15 minutes) and then add in the other star – the cooked lentils. Mix this all in and ensure everything is to your taste! Then garnish with coriander and serve.

TIP: If you have the time, try cooking more than one lentil type (such as moong lentils and black lentils) and incorporate these into the dish. The variety of lentils tips the curry into a beautiful blend of sweet yet savoury flavours.

DAAL BEGUN GATTA

THICCCCC SWEET AND SOUR TOFU PATHIA

THICCCCC SWEET AND SOUR TOFU PATHIA

Serves: **3-4 people**

Prep: **15 minutes**

Cook: **20 minutes**

INGREDIENTS

600g firm tofu, diced into bite-size pieces

2 teaspoons cumin seeds

1 teaspoon fenugreek seeds

An oil of your choice

2 brown onions, sliced

40g fresh ginger, peeled and grated

5 garlic cloves, crushed

2 teaspoons garam masala

3 tablespoons tomato puree

1½ tins/cartons of chopped tomatoes

Water

2 teaspoons turmeric

1 teaspoon chilli powder

My Pathia is a one-stop-darling-eat-your-heart-out dish. Very succulent, loaded balls of tofu are surrounded by a deliciously sweet sauce, with a hint of sourness provided by a thick creamy soy yogurt base. A vibrant, sweet dish, I was proud when I tasted the result! The Pathia has a lot of steps, though, because it's almost two parts to the dish. Thirteen-year-old me, eat your heart out!

INSTRUCTIONS

We'll cook the tofu first, in the oven. Bake the tofu pieces in the oven at 200°C in a greased baking tray lined with parchment paper. Let these pieces cook for around 15-18 minutes.

Once cooked, we can get straight to the sauce and seasoning! Get a pan over medium heat and add the onions, garlic, and ginger. Season the pan with the cumin and fenugreek seeds for some aroma, and let the onions swelter away until they are golden brown. Let all the ingredients soften together; if you need to add water to soften them further, add dashes of cold water and reduce the sauce.

The above method is the bhuna cooking method, where you cook and season everything in the pan as you go along. However, because we don't want the tofu to overcook, we're going to season the pan and then mix the tofu into the pan. So, in the reduced onions, add the garam masala, curry powder, and all-purpose seasoning. Add the chopped tomatoes, puree, turmeric, and chilli powder, and mix the flavours all in! Then stir in your dollops of soy yogurt; this will bring out the hint of sourness in the dish!

Continued on page 48…

47

2 teaspoons all-purpose seasoning

---

2 teaspoons curry powder

---

2 dollops of coconut/soy yogurt

150g of garden peas/petit pois (the latter is sweeter)

¼ teaspoon salt

---

2 tablespoons light brown sugar

Coriander

Get the cooked tofu out of the oven, add it to your pan, and add in the peas. Mix well, then add salt and pepper to taste as well as the brown sugar, and combine everything well. Let this mixture simmer in the pan for ten minutes.

Garnish with coriander – serve with whatever sides you like!

TIP: Towards the end of the dish (once the colour of the sauce begins to take shape), slowly add the brown sugar into the dish, stir, taste, and repeat. Sugar is the most significant contributor of sweetness in this curry, so make it as sweet as you are!

THE FULL-BODIED COURGETTE CURRY

INGREDIENTS

1/3 cup (79 ml) olive oil

2 medium onions, thinly sliced

3 teaspoons of ginger-garlic paste

1 teaspoon cumin seeds

1 medium tomato, cubed

Salt and pepper to taste

1 teaspoon coriander powder

1 teaspoon chilli powder

3 large courgettes sliced into small rectangular chunks

2 green chillies, slit

1 Naga chilli, cut in half

½ teaspoon turmeric powder

Coriander to garnish

Courgettes are a bit dull. Small and green, but people still have trouble determining what they bring to the table. However, combine them with some beautiful earthy flavours which bring out an excellent taste to the courgettes, and have them entwined with aroma and flavour from the caramelised onion, and you have a fantastic dish!

INSTRUCTIONS

You know the drill! Get the oil in a pan over medium heat. Once the oil is hot, drop in the onions (they should sizzle when they're in) and cook until translucent. Now add your garlic. Once you have done this, add in all your dry spices except the turmeric, and stir through for about 2 minutes.

Turn the heat down to medium-low (we don't want the onions sticking!) and add the tomatoes. After a minute of stirring, add in the courgettes, too! Salt and pepper to your taste before adding about 50ml of water and stir to ensure everything is well coated.

Now, this is up to you: either break the courgettes into small pieces using your wooden spoon, or continue cooking in chinks. Add the turmeric and slice in the chillies. Continue to stir!

Now turn the heat to low; we'll cook everything well here, so leave on low heat for about 18 minutes, stirring occasionally. If courgettes start sticking to the pan at any point, add some water and boil it off on a high heat. Continue to salt and pepper to taste, as water can dilute the flavour.

After this, garnish with coriander and enjoy!

NO BUTTER, NO CHICKEN CURRY

Serves: **3-4 people**
600g extra firm tofu

Prep: **25 minutes**

Cook: **30 minutes**

INGREDIENTS

For the tofu marinade:

⅔ cup raw cashews (100g)

⅓ cup water (80ml)

A squeeze of half a lemon

2 teaspoons garam masala

1 teaspoon chilli powder

1 teaspoon all-purpose seasoning

2 tablespoons vegan butter

I set this as a challenge to myself when I realised that a few friends had started turning vegan but loved their butter chicken! So, one night after the end of my shift, I got to cooking. Made with tofu and cashews, this deliciously creamy dish has a beautifully sweet, nutty flavour. 'No Butter, No Chicken' is a perfect harmony of sweetness and spice. We'll make our vegan marinade here, too, to bring out the creaminess and colour of the dish.

INSTRUCTIONS

If you've done the other tofu recipes in this book, you know we get the tofu cooking first! Preheat the oven to 200°C. Chop the tofu into small cube pieces, about an inch in length, and place them into a mixing bowl. We're going to marinade this soon.

In a food processor, add the cashews, a squeeze of a lemon, some salt and garam masala, and the other dry spices. Blend until it becomes a smooth marinade, and then pour this beautiful mixture over the tofu in the mixing bowl. Mix well (make sure all the nooks and crannies are seasoned!) and transfer onto a baking tray lined with parchment paper. Bake at 200°C in the preheated oven for about 15-18 minutes until the tofu cooks.

Continued on page 52...

The curry sauce

2 tablespoons vegan butter

---

1 medium brown onion, diced finely

---

1 heaped teaspoon of fenugreek seeds

---

5 cloves crushed garlic

---

3 bay leaves

---

1 tablespoon ginger, freshly grated

---

1 tablespoon garam masala

---

2 teaspoon turmeric

---

2 teaspoon cumin

---

1 teaspoon cayenne pepper

---

1 cup crushed tomatoes (240ml)

---

1 cup canned coconut cream (240ml), unsweetened

½ tablespoon light brown sugar

Salt and pepper to taste

As the tofu is cooking, you can start on the sauce! Add vegan butter to the pan and let that melt away (do not let it brown, as then you'll burn the butter!), drop in the onions, and let them svelte away. Once the onions soften, add the garlic, bay leaves, and cloves, and let these toast. Then add the rest of the powdered spices and mix around. Once the dish colours, drop in the tomatoes and coconut cream, and stir well. Let this come to a simmer, and as it reduces, dash in the sugar (maybe do it like Salt Bae, cause it's fiiineee!). Add the tofu pieces, stir them in, and mix well. Garnish with coriander!

Tip: Add some chickpeas to texture the dish; chickpeas are lovely.

NO BUTTER, NO CHICKEN CURRY

THE VEGAN BRUMMIE BALTI

INGREDIENTS

400ml of vegan curry base

1 red onion, finely diced for the base

½ onion, sliced for the sauce

½ red pepper, sliced

½ green pepper, sliced

2 teaspoons oil

3 bay leaves

6 pieces of cloves

1 black cardamom pod

3 green cardamom pods

1 cup of cubed sweet potato, parboiled

Salt and pepper to taste

3 teaspoons coriander seeds, or use ground coriander

So, Balti means bucket in about four different languages. The story is that a curry house in 1980s Birmingham used to cook this dish in a bucket (a 'Balti'), and that's where the name of the dish came from. Somehow, word spread, and about a decade later, this bucket-inspired dish was in restaurants across the UK. There was no chance I would not include a proper vegan version in my book! But don't worry, I've made sure to bring the complete and true flavour to the Balti here, in all its glory.

INSTRUCTIONS

First thing's first: we're going to make a spice mix. Take the (deep breath now!) coriander seeds, ground cumin, ground cardamom, fenugreek seeds, cinnamon, chilli powder, curry powder, and garam masala, and combine all of these in a small bowl. Grind everything together with a pestle and mortar. Set this aside and keep it in high regard, as this brings all the flavour to the Balti!

In a pan, get oil in over medium heat. Once the pan gets hot, add the diced red onions and let these become translucent. Then add your dry spices (i.e. cloves, cardamom pods, and bay leaves) and toast the spices in the pan. Add the pre-boiled sweet potato to the Balti and let these fry so the inside of them is cooked, but the outside is textured. Then drop in your spice mix and stir!

Continued on page 56…

1 teaspoon ground cumin

1 teaspoon ground cardamom

½ teaspoon of fenugreek seeds

½ teaspoon cinnamon

1 teaspoon chilli powder

1 teaspoon curry powder

1 teaspoon garam masala

Coriander to garnish

Mint to garnish

Now add in your sliced onions and peppers, and cook away the rawness without making the sliced vegetables lose their shape, so they retain a crunch.

As everything simmers, take a minute to admire your spice mix before adding the vegan curry base to the pan. Cover the pan to let all the vegetables cook for around 5 minutes. Take the lid off, stir, and leave on a simmer until you are ready to serve! Garnish with coriander and mint!

BINDI DAAL GATTA

Serves: **3-4 people**

Prep: **20 minutes**

Cook: **35 minutes**

INGREDIENTS

1½ cups water

½ cup brown lentils

1 teaspoon turmeric

1 teaspoon chilli powder

1 teaspoon garam masala

1 teaspoon curry powder

2 teaspoons all-purpose seasoning

1 teaspoon cumin powder

A pinch of salt, plus more to taste

1 14oz can diced tomatoes

2 tablespoons coconut cream

1 tablespoon tamarind paste

1 tablespoon oil

3 bay leaves

1 small onion, chopped

2 teaspoons garam masala

2 cups chopped okra

Chopped coriander to garnish

Another staple of the restaurant is a variation of the Gatta dish. Like before, we still incorporate a plethora of lentil types into this dish, but we use the okra's runny texture and sweetness to provide a distinctly different taste! Bindi Daal Gatta is another popular dish at my restaurant. I am including this one especially for the customers who always request the recipe!

INSTRUCTIONS

(This dish requires a few more pans than usual!)

We'll start with getting the lentils out of the way! Letting these cook saves time as we move onto other things! Rinse the lentils in cold running water (we don't need to get ill!), then drain and set aside. To cook them, bring a pan of water to a boil, drop the lentils in with a pinch of salt and turmeric, stir, and let this cook for about 25 minutes.

Once the lentils are tender, we'll drain them and set them aside. Then, add tomatoes, coconut cream, and tamarind paste to the pan. Let these simmer before adding the lentils back in to absorb the pleasant, sweet taste. Lentils – done!

With the okra, get another pan and heat oil over medium heat. Add bay leaves, cloves, and pepper, and toast these spices in the oil. Once you get an aroma, drop in the chopped onions and let these sauté away! Once the onions brown, add garam masala and the rest of the dry spices. Stir everything in, and then add the chopped okra (this provides the heat!). Continue stirring until the okra soften, which should take around 5-7 minutes!

Now grab the other pan and combine the two – hence your Bindi Daal. Stir everything in well, add salt and pepper to taste (it will need around 3 teaspoons), and make sure all the flavours become well acquainted! Garnish with coriander, and serve with rice/roti!

TIP: Try and keep the okra as dry as you can; if the okra holds too much water, it becomes more mushy – to the point where it's not pleasant.

MINGLING AND MIXING VEGETABLE JALFREZI

Serves: **3-4 people**

Prep: **25 minutes**

Cook: **20 minutes**

INGREDIENTS

1 large aubergine

4 tablespoons sunflower or olive oil

2 onions (one deep fried in vegetable oil for 15 mins, and sliced into half-moons)

1 red pepper

Small bunch of fresh coriander

5 green Bird's-Eye chillies

12 cherry tomatoes

3 tablespoons curry powder

1 teaspoon garam masala

½-2 teaspoons hot chilli powder

8 tablespoons tomato purée

Salt

2 teaspoons ginger-garlic paste

5 garlic cloves

500ml + 1 tablespoon water

Continued on page 60…

The Jalfrezi is a silky, spicy dish with a runny sauce peppered with… well, literally peppers. Peppers, onions, and spice are all in a beautiful dish that packs a zing of heat for your tongue. You could make this spicy dish medium, by easing up on the chilli and curry powder! As we make a vegan variant, we're going to drop in some thick, girthy aubergines to bring some thickness to the dish.

INSTRUCTIONS

Right, first things first, let's get the oven warm at 190°C so we can roast our aubergine. Cut the aubergine into nice, chunky, and thick pieces (about 2cms). Place into a baking tray, drizzle with olive oil, and season them with salt. Mix around and stick in the oven until golden brown (it'll take approximately 18 minutes).

While cooking the aubergine, you can start on the 'masala' (the vegan curry base). Please take one of the 2 onions and finely chop it. Take a pan, pour in a glug of oil over medium heat, and let it heat up. Once the pan has reached adequate heat, drop in the onions and ginger-garlic paste. Afterwards, drop in the red chillies, and let all of this toast for five minutes.

Now add the powdered spices that bring the flavour! Stir until the onions change colour because of the spices. Once the onions reduce, add about 500 ml of water, and let this simmer. Take the mixture off the heat and blend it until the mixture becomes a lovely smooth liquid – this is your masala! Set this spicy liquid to the side and return to the other cooking that needs doing.

3 cherry tomatoes

2 fresh red chillies

1 Naga chilli, sliced into two

3 green chillies

1 teaspoon ground coriander

1 teaspoon ground cumin

1 teaspoon ground fenugreek

1 teaspoon ground turmeric

2 teaspoons chilli powder

Slice some onions carefully into thick slices, slice your pepper into nice large slices (make sure to keep the pepper seeds, PLEASE), and chop some coriander. Slit three chillies so that they also retain their seeds, and quarter your tomatoes.

Get the pan back and place it on high heat. Add what you have just chopped, which is the onion, pepper, and sliced chillies, and pan-fry these for about 5 minutes. Stir in the chopped coriander stems and the remaining ginger-garlic paste. Add the curry powder, garam masala, ¼ teaspoon hot chilli powder, tomato purée, and grilled aubergines. Let these all simmer but retain some thickness so that they don't overcook, and then add your luscious masala! Mix everything well and let it simmer for 5 minutes.

Garnish with sliced chillies and coriander!

Tip: Take the time to cut onions and peppers into half-moon shapes – I promise you, it's worth it.

RUBY VEGAN BHUNA

INGREDIENTS

2 teaspoons curry powder

1 teaspoon chilli powder

1 teaspoon paprika

1 teaspoon fenugreek seeds

½ teaspoon kosher salt

3 tablespoons oil

½ onion, coarsely chopped

2 green chillies, seeded and diced (or thinly sliced if you want a bit of extra heat from the ribs)

1 tablespoon coriander stems, minced

1 tablespoon garlic-ginger paste

2 tablespoons tomato paste, with enough water to dilute to the consistency of the dish

Vegan curry base
(see page 117 for recipe)

12ozs extra firm tofu

1 tablespoon tamarind sauce

3-4 cherry tomatoes, cut in half

Bhuna isn't a dish. It's a method of cooking which is one-pot – no liquidiser or extra steps needed. Yet, for some reason (there must have been some translation issues), it is its own dish over here in the UK. It's been one of the most popular dishes in Ruby Murrays across the UK, so here's my recipe for our Bhuna dish, cooked just like in the restaurant.

INSTRUCTIONS

Oven preheated at 200°C.

Okay, so with restaurant-style cooking, first you will not prep the vegetables but prep your spice mix. Place all the powdered spices on a plate and mix them, then leave them on the plate to use when you're cooking.

Stick your extra-firm tofu in the oven at 200°C and let it cook for 18 minutes, until it starts to brown.

Get a pan over medium heat and add your oil. As it simmers, drop in your chopped onions and let them brown. As they turn translucent, add your garlic-ginger paste and stir it in! Add your tomato paste and mix this in, too. Now drop in the spice mix! Let this mix in the pan, and then add about 3ozs of your vegan curry base.

Let this simmer, then add another 6ozs of vegan curry base to make your sauce flavoured and perfect for a Bhuna. Add some tamarind sauce, then turn the heat down to low, and add your cooked tofu! Mix well, and make sure the tofu is coated well with that Bhuna flavour! Let the curry come to a simmer, and 4 minutes before finishing, drop in your chopped cherry tomatoes.

Garnish with coriander.

IF JOSH WAS INDIAN – VEGAN ROGAN

INGREDIENTS

2 tablespoons olive oil
(you can use vegetable
oil if you prefer)

1 medium brown onion,
peeled, cut in half lengthways,
then sliced thinly

½ teaspoon sea salt,

10 green cardamom pods

2 teaspoons cumin seeds

½ teaspoon fennel seeds

2 teaspoon ginger-garlic paste

2 teaspoons paprika

2 teaspoons ground coriander

½ teaspoon garam masala

½ scant teaspoon dried red
chilli flakes

1 tablespoon tomato purée
(paste)

1 large aubergine, cut into
bite-size pieces

Continued on page 64…

A standard Ruby Murray dish, this has been supporting curry restaurants since the 1960s. There's nothing wrong with keeping a classic in the cookbook, but don't worry, I've made it special; I've made it personal, and I've made it vegan!

INSTRUCTIONS

Heat the oil in a large sauté pan over medium heat. Drop in the onion, some salt, 10 green cardamom pods, 10 black peppercorns, 2 teaspoons of cumin seeds, and ½ teaspoon of fennel seeds. We're going to let these toast and provide some fragrance. Keep cooking the onions until they become translucent. Add some ginger-garlic paste and the chilli flakes; this will give some spice before we add more spices! Add in the ground coriander, 2 teaspoons of chilli powder, and 2 teaspoons of garam masala. Stir and cook for a minute until they release their aromas too.

Next, drop in just one tablespoon of tomato paste (please no more than one, because tomato puree overpowers dishes with a tomato flavour; this isn't Italian cooking!) Also, add in about ¼ of a cup of cold water, and stir this all together to make your vegan curry base.

Add your chopped aubergine and pepper to the pan, stirring them in well. Turn off the heat and add soy yogurt, tomatoes, and chickpeas. Again, add another ¼ cup of water and stir it well with the spice mix to let it all 'cook out'.

1 large green bell pepper, pith and seeds removed, then chopped into large pieces

---

150g/½ a cup soy yogurt

14.5oz can of chopped tomatoes

---

1 cup water, divided into 2 equal portions

15oz can cooked chickpeas (240g drained weight)

---

1 cinnamon stick

---

2 dried bay leaves

---

1 green chilli, slit, for garnish

---

1 slice of lime, for garnish

Afterwards, drop in a stick of cinnamon and three bay leaves. Cover the pan with a lid and cook over low-medium heat for 15 minutes. Then drop in the chopped coriander and cook until the aubergine is soft and your sauce is thick and creamy (to make it thicker, add in a tiny bit more aubergine, salt, and taste!).

IF JOSH WAS INDIAN — VEGAN ROGAN

I'M IN LOVE WITH THE COCO CURRY

I'M IN LOVE WITH THE COCO CURRY

Serves: **3-4 people**

Prep: **15 minutes**

Cook: **15 minutes**

INGREDIENTS

1 tablespoon of oil

3 bay leaves

Shredded coconut (loose, about 10-20gs based on preference)

10 cloves

2 cinnamon sticks

5 green cardamom pods

1 cup cauliflower

1 onion, finely diced

1 sweet potato, parboiled and salted

2 carrots

½ zucchini

2 teaspoons curry powder

2 teaspoons all-purpose seasoning

Continued on page 68…

Something sweet, something different, something… easy? This dish is probably one of the simplest dishes in the book. Whack everything into a pan, stir it together, and then taste your perfection. Literally! If you explore all areas of Indian cuisine, the sweetness of the coconut paired with the thickness of the sauce puts this dish in its own league. It's very different, too, by incorporating vegetables like cauliflower and carrots. If you're nutty about coconut, whip out your pan and knife and get to cooking it up in the kitchen!

INSTRUCTIONS

This dish needs very little skill, so it's the perfect beginner's recipe. Grate the carrots into nice shreds and chop the potato into chunks. Then chop the cauliflower and zucchini; these vegetables thicken the dish. That is your main prep work done!

Get a pan out, add some olive oil and let it warm over medium heat. Add your diced onions and begin toasting the dry spices to give some aroma (cinnamon sticks, bay leaves, green cardamom, and cloves). Once the dry spices are toasted, add your vegan curry base and all the dry spices listed. Stir this around in the pan so your kitchen smells nice (hopefully, there's someone there to compliment you!).

1 teaspoon garam masala

½ teaspoon of vegan curry base (see page 117 for my version!)

---

1 200ml can of coconut milk

---

1 300ml can of chickpeas

---

1 tablespoon honey

Salt and pepper to taste

Squeeze of a lime

---

3 lime wedges, for garnish

Add your coconut milk, honey, and salt to your taste. Mix well together and let this simmer for about 7 minutes. Once it's all mixed in, garnish it with shredded coconut, coriander, and some lime wedges!

TU MOTA KADDU (YOU FAT PUMPKIN)

Serves: **3-4 people**

Prep: **15 minutes**

Cook: **25 minutes**

INGREDIENTS

4 tablespoons oil

2 cinnamon sticks

6 green cardamom pods

1 black cardamom pod

2 cinnamon sticks

¼ cup mixed nuts

450 grams pumpkin, cubed

1 mango, sliced

1 inch ginger piece

3 green chillies

2 tablespoons coriander, finely chopped

1 teaspoon fenugreek seeds

1 teaspoon salt, or adjust to taste

1 teaspoon turmeric powder

When I was younger, I used to be chubby (fat, if you wanted to be mean to me), and my cousins would never let me hear the end of it! I used to get called 'Kaddu' a lot as a tease, even by my mum when I used to go into the kitchen and eat three bags of crisps in one go. To be honest, I'm glad, as she also showed me this recipe – a kaddu-based dish that I can't help but overeat to this day. With the delectable sweetness provided by the pumpkin (and some mango, because mango is mmmm), the use of spices gives this dish a perfect balance of taste and sweetness, with the latter hitting you first with every mouthful. And don't be fooled by the name of the dish! Pumpkin is incredibly filling and healthy!

INSTRUCTIONS

I've said it so often that it should be second nature by now, so bring out a pan over medium heat and add some oil. Let that heat up, and then add some dry spices (bay leaves, green cardamom, black cardamom, and cinnamon). Toast these spices up! We'll also add some extra things here before we carry on, so drop in the fenugreek seeds, the chilli, and ginger. These will all give a different aroma to the dish!

Drop the nuts and pumpkins into the dish (pumpkin takes time to cook). Salt your pumpkin and add some turmeric to give the dish a nice colour and bring an 'earthy' taste. Cover with a lid and let this cook out for two minutes.

Add in a dash of cold water (about 50ml) after two minutes, then stir and cover again for ten minutes. Give it a nice stir every five minutes, and repeat until the pumpkin becomes a bit soft. If you need to keep adding dashes of cold water, do!

Continued on page 70…

1 teaspoon red chilli powder/
cayenne pepper

---

1 tablespoon coriander powder

---

1 tablespoon crushed fennel
seeds

---

2 tablespoons brown sugar

---

1 teaspoon garam masala

Finally, add the raw mango and all the powdered spices listed above to bring a depth of sweetness and flavour. Mix well together, so everything gets to know each other – bit like speed dating! Add some salt and brown sugar to your taste, and garnish with roasted cashew nuts.

TIP: If the pumpkin is too hard to cut into chunks, try roasting it in the oven with a bit of salt for 10 minutes at about 120°C, the pumpkin should become more tender, but not so much that it becomes mushy!

TU MOTA KADDU (YOU FAT PUMPKIN)

BEGUN URIBEESHI GATTA

BEGUN URIBEESHI GATTA

Serves: **3-4 people**

Prep: **15 minutes**

Cook: **25 minutes**

INGREDIENTS

2 cups water

¼ cup olive oil

1 medium aubergine, cut into ½ inch cubes

1 onion, diced

3 garlic cloves, minced

2 green chillies, slit

2 teaspoons garam masala to taste

1 teaspoon chilli powder

2 teaspoons curry powder

1 teaspoon ground cumin

1 cup of navy beans

9ozs of vegan curry base

Salt and pepper to taste

2 teaspoons garlic-ginger paste

Continued on page 74…

This recipe isn't straight from the restaurant; it was perfected by my great-grandmother a century ago in my motherland – a rural village in Bangladesh. A testament to the staple Bengali runner beans, Uribeeshi has fed Bengalis since Noah began inviting animals to join him on his boat tour. Look no further if you want a truly authentic, pan-fried Bengali dish. Begun Uribeeshi Gatta brims with flavour, provided by spicing the beans and pairing them with cooked aubergine to give a very distinctive taste.

INSTRUCTIONS

Okay, let's get some beauty on a dish started. Start by bringing out your pan, pour in the olive oil and get it over medium heat. Next, get the spices toasted, so drop in the bay leaves, cloves, and both colours of the cardamom into your pan. Now add in your garlic. Once you hear the spices pop as they're toasted, drop in your chopped onion! Cook away until the onions turn translucent, and then add your ginger-garlic paste. Mix in well and let the distinct aroma of the ginger-garlic paste hit your nose!

Drop in the dry spices to colour the dish – it should change into a beautiful shade of red – and let this cook for a minute before adding in your aubergines and beans. Let these cook

2 teaspoons of tomato puree

2 bay leaves

3 cloves

2 black cardamom

4 green cardamom

¼ cup chopped fresh coriander

away for approximately 5 minutes until cooked, but not so much that the aubergine begins to lose shape. Then add 3ozs of the vegan curry base and reduce the heat. Add your tomato puree and salt and pepper to your taste! Stir until it comes to a simmer, at which point add the rest of the vegan curry base!

Garnish with coriander (optional)!

THE SHAHI SAHAKARI THALI

Serves: **4-5 people**

Prep: **45 minutes**

Cook: **60 minutes**

Thali is the one to impress. Do you have friends over and want to show them the power of plants? Use this dish. Need to impress a date? Use this dish. Need to convince your boss that you shouldn't be fired for sleeping on the job? Use. This. Dish. Shahi Sahakari Thali is my restaurant's flagship vegan dish. It involves batch cooking previous recipes in the book, and presenting everything in one illustrious Thali platter. Served with roti and rice, it truly is a dish that takes you across the vegan subcontinent. Even though this dish has no cooking instructions, it takes recipes from previous pages and encompasses them on one platter.

This dish takes a lot of time! So maybe do it when you are cooking for multiple people!

P.S. You may need to buy a Thali platter, which you can purchase online!

INSTRUCTIONS

Right, what you need to do is take the recipes from the list below, and cook them in separate pans as if you were cooking them on their own.

Complete the recipe list for Uribeeshi Biran

Complete the recipe list for Bombay Aloo

Complete the recipe list for Begun Daal Gatta

Complete the recipe list for Chowle Achar

Complete the recipe list for Roti

Cook some rice which is enough for the number of people present

Then on Thali platters, carefully put each dish into one cup so that each Thali has a small portion of each dish. Then complete the Thali with a cup of rice and a chapati per person. Garnish the curry dishes with sliced coriander.

Shahi Sahakari Thali translates into 'the vegan king', with the idea that this platter is fit for a king from City Spice, the King of Brick Lane. If you are confident in cooking from the recipes in this dish, then definitely attempt this!

PART THREE:
MAIN COURSES

DRY

THE ONLY TIME BEING DRY IS A GOOD THING

JACKFRUIT BENGALI BIRIYANI

INGREDIENTS

As it's a Biriyani dish, which can be a bit more complicated to cook, I've split the ingredients list into three to make this easier:

For the rice:

300g basmati rice

2 teaspoons salt

Squeeze of ½ a lemon

For the jackfruit:

Oil for frying

2 tins of canned jackfruit

3 teaspoons ginger-garlic paste

Salt and pepper to taste

1 teaspoon ground turmeric

1 teaspoon chilli powder

1 teaspoon paprika

1 teaspoon cumin powder

Continued on page 80…

Let me show you my personal favourite Biriyani dish. Cook this well and the myriad of flavours from the meaty-texture jackfruit will hypnotise you, and you will be mesmerised by the desi-spiced rice and potatoes. For me, this is the perfect Biriyani dish – and its heralded Bengali family recipe, refined by me, is perfection in Biriyani cooking.

INSTRUCTIONS

Okay, let's get the rice cooking. First, wash it and leave it in a bowl, soaked in water. Please wash your rice as unnecessary starch is like a wart – no-one benefits from it.

Grab your jackfruit from the tin, drain it, and remove as much water as possible! Add everything in that section of the ingredients in a mixing bowl and mix well. Let the jackfruit learn new things by mixing with the flavours. Leave the bowl in the fridge for at least 30 minutes, preferably overnight (make sure to cover it with clingfilm!).

Preheat your oven to 200°C and put in your potatoes to bake for 10-15 minutes until golden brown. (Leave the oven on!). Salt your potatoes before inserting into the oven. After they cook, set aside. Once cool, slice into very small chunks.

The best way to use the jackfruit is to deep fry it, so get a pot, get some oil sizzling at 180°C, and drop in the seasoned jackfruit individually, making sure not to cluster the pan! Otherwise, the oil will spit back and scar you! Cooking the jackfruit will take one minute over frying heat.

For the biryani:

150g baby potatoes, cut into bite-sized chunks

Oil for cooking

2 crispy fried onions, sliced into half-moons (fry in 250ml vegetable oil for 15 minutes)

3 teaspoons ginger-garlic paste

Salt and pepper to taste

1 teaspoon chilli powder

2 teaspoons cumin powder

1 teaspoon curry powder

1 teaspoon garam masala

Squeeze of a lemon

150g full-fat soy yogurt (obviously vegan)

2 green chillies, cut into slices

50g vegan butter

Combine all the ingredients in the biryani ingredient section, then add the potatoes and jackfruit as your base. Cook your rice in a separate bowl until it is about 75% done, then drain and transfer this rice onto your biriyani base. Over the rice, add saffron and the squeeze of lemon. Then break up the vegan butter and put knobs of the butter around the edge of the pan. Transfer to the oven at 200°C and let it cook for 20 minutes.

After this, take the dish out and let it stand for 5 minutes, so it cools. Garnish with mint and extra slices of jackfruit!

TIP: if you are a beginner, there is nothing wrong with cooking the rice about 80% through in a rice cooker. The last thing you want is the rice to be too soggy when making the biriyani – and I don't want soggy rice putting you off cooking!

JACKFRUIT BENGALI BIRIYANI

GOOD GOLLY GOBI ACHARI

GOOD GOLLY GOBI ACHARI

Serves: **3-4 people**

Prep: **25 minutes**

Cook: **15 minutes**

INGREDIENTS

Divided into two sections for clarity:

Section a:

3 dry red chillies

1 teaspoon fenugreek seeds

2 bay leaves

6 cloves

1 black cardamom

2 teaspoons cumin powder

Squeeze of a lemon

Section b:

½ teaspoon nigella seeds

½ teaspoon mustard seeds

1-inch cinnamon stick

Bite-size florets of 1 cauliflower

2 medium red onions, thinly sliced

Continued on page 84…

'Cauliflowers marinated in a beautiful blend of spices and pickle. Tangy and incredibly distinct in flavour, the pickle blend will bring a refreshing experience to your palate.' I wrote this when I designed the menu for an eatery I used to work in when I was 14. I'll be honest, this Punjabi-based dish comes out all guns blazing with its sharp, tangy taste. A wonderful delight with very little sauce, it's a sure-fire way to try and like new things.

INSTRUCTIONS

Okay, the first thing we do here is make a spice paste, so take the dry spices mentioned above and toast them in a pan. Then transfer into a mortar and pestle and add the cumin powder. Use the mortar and pestle to grind the spices into a fine powder, squeeze the lemon juice over it and use a teaspoon of what is now our pickle to be utilised later. (Only use ingredients in section a.)

Then, get a pan over medium heat, add a glug of oil, and begin cooking the cauliflower florets along with the onions. Salt them in the pan, and after ten minutes, add the garlic-ginger paste to the seeds and cook until the sliced onions soften. Mix the dish well together, then drop in the tomato paste. Now you can add the flavour and pour the

1 tablespoon tomato paste

1 tablespoon of ginger-garlic
paste

2 tablespoons soy yogurt

1 teaspoon sugar

3 green chillies (optional)

Oil

Salt

pickle mix all over the cauliflower in the pan until the florets are very well coloured. Let the cauliflowers cook through. Add a dash of water (50ml) and mix the pan. Let the water reduce and drop in soy yogurt, slit green chillies (optional), and enjoy!

THE VEGAN MIX GRILL

Serves: **2-3 people**

Prep: **30 minutes**

Cook: **15-20 minutes**

An array of vegetables and tofu, roasted in a cacophony of Indian spices, and you have a platter fit for a king. Serve straight from the oven, or use a grill to get that beautiful char, this is a dish that would make meat meaningless even to the staunchest carnivore. Pair it up with dollops of lovely mint sauce and mango chutney, and you will never look back.

INSTRUCTIONS

We are going to approach this very similarly to the Thali. We want to create a massive platter of flavour, love, and spice, incorporating a select number of dry dishes already seen in this book. Take the recipes from the list below, cook them in separate pans, and make a fantastic platter of food!

Complete the recipe list for Cumin Potatoes

Complete the recipe list for Sammy's kebab

Complete the recipe list for the Tofu Tikka Skewers

Complete the recipe list for So Good So Popular Onion Bhajis

In addition, season some sliced onions with salt, 1 teaspoon all-purpose seasoning, and ½ teaspoon turmeric, and pan fry these on a high heat for 15 minutes. These onions go great with any grilled dishes!

Once everything is cooked, serve on a huge platter. Arrange it how you would like and then drizzle generously with vegan mint sauce, raita, and mango chutney!

And then feast!

TOFU BIRIYANI

Serves: **3-4 people**

Prep: **40 minutes**

Cook: **40 minutes**

INGREDIENTS

1½ cups basmati rice
(washed in running water)

2 dry bay leaves

6 cloves

6 green cardamom pods

1-inch piece cinnamon

2 black cardamom pods

2 teaspoon cumin seeds

1 tablespoon vegetable oil

2 medium carrots (finely
diced, so they cook quickly)

2 medium potatoes (finely
diced)

2 heaped teaspoons ginger-
garlic paste

Coriander

1½ cups vegan yogurt

Continued on page 88…
Continued on page 88…

Like our Jackfruit Bengali Biriyani, this one packs a punch! A lightly spiced, rice-based dish filled with tofu and a lot of hearty, chunky vegetables, this is a Biriyani that will get anyone drooling after the first bite. The best thing is, this Biriyani is a breeze to cook, with very little prep work needed! Biriyani on a lazy Sunday, anyone?

INSTRUCTIONS

We're going to start with the rice: wash your rice (seriously), and then in a pot, add 2 cups of water for every cup of rice you've used (or if you know how to, use your fingers to measure). Then add three cardamom pods (green and black), bay leaves, and cinnamon. Also, add three cloves and a teaspoon of cumin seeds. You are doing this to make the rice smell amazing and bring out some of the flavour. Salt the water, get it boiling, and once it simmers, put the lid over the pot and let the rice cook until it is three-quarters done.

As the rice is cooking, we can now prep our vegetables. By this, I mean chop them. And then, as usual, get a pan with oil over medium heat. Once the oil gets hot, drop in the rest of your dry spices and start toasting them! Release that fragrance into your kitchen!

Drop in your chopped carrots and potatoes and season with salt and black pepper. Cover the pan and let these cook through (will take about 5 minutes). Now we're going to add the ginger-garlic paste, coriander, and mint, and stir them in. Add your tofu, the soy yogurt, and then your dry powders, and stir these in too. Add the rice over your newly-formed Biriyani base, and then sprinkle in the fried onions and

2 heaped tablespoons
garam masala

---

2 teaspoons chilli powder

---

1 teaspoon curry powder

---

1 teaspoon paprika

---

1 teaspoon turmeric

---

1 teaspoon coriander powder

½ cup raw cashew nuts

12-14ozs extra-firm tofu
(cut into small cubes)

Salt and ground black
pepper to taste

---

3 green chillies, slit

Fried onions, for garnish

Roasted cashew nuts,
for garnish

---

cashews. Stick this pan into the oven for 15 minutes at 200°C or until the rice is fully cooked.

Get a large wooden spoon, mix the rice and base together, and there you have it! Delicious Tofu Biriyani! Garnish with roasted cashew nuts and some fried onions for crunch!

TIP: Just like the previous Biriyani dish, if you are a beginner, there is nothing wrong with cooking the rice at about 80% in a rice cooker. The last thing you want is the rice to be too soggy when making the Biriyani – and I don't want to put you off cooking!

TOFU BIRIYANI

PART FOUR: SIDE DISHES AND SAUCES

NOTHING WRONG WITH HAVING A FEW SAUCY SIDE TINGS...

CUMIN POTATOES

INGREDIENTS

4 potatoes, peeled, boiled, and cubed

1 red onion, diced finely

2 tablespoons vegetable oil

1 tablespoon coriander seeds

2 teaspoons cumin seeds

2 green chillies, slit lengthways

3cms fresh ginger, sliced very thinly

1 teaspoon red chilli powder

½ teaspoon turmeric powder

Salt and pepper to taste

2 teaspoons mango powder (amchoor powder)

Fried onions, for garnish.

Earthy, rich in flavour, and tangy - cumin potatoes are a lovely side dish for some sour yet spicy additions to your palate! A perfect companion to a vegan curry dish (such as the Pathia) with a glass of Merlot; the combination is heavenly.

INSTRUCTIONS

We'll get started, as usual, by getting a pot hot with salted water and dropping in your taters! The potatoes will take about ten minutes to boil. Once the potatoes boil, chop them up into 4cm cubes (but you can swap this around if you want, and chop them before cooking).

In a pan, toast one teaspoon coriander seeds and one teaspoon cumin seeds until your kitchen becomes fragrant. Then transfer these spices into a mortar and pestle and get crushing! Let them cool for health and safety reasons.

In the pan, drop in some oil and add the remainder of the seeds. Stir in the sliced onions until translucent, and then drop in the green chillies and sliced ginger. As these sauté, decrease the heat from medium to low, and add the rest of the dry spices and potatoes. Salt and pepper to taste, and mix! Make sure the potatoes properly coat in the seasoning!

Serve only the potatoes, and garnish with some fried onions!

Toast a glass of red wine to yourself to say well done!

PROPER PALONG SAAG

Serves: **3-4 people**

Prep: **15 minutes**

Cook: **15 minutes**

INGREDIENTS

3 teaspoons of ginger-garlic paste

2 to 3 green chillies, minced

Oil for frying

1 onion, finely chopped

1 heaped teaspoon salt

1 heaped teaspoon garam masala

1 level teaspoon of turmeric powder

1 level teaspoon of ground cumin

1 heaped teaspoon of ground coriander

500g fresh spinach, best with oversized leaves, roughly chopped

1 teaspoon dried fenugreek leaves

½ lemon, juiced

Green/red chillies, for garnish

The best thing about side dishes is that they are effortless to cook, yet are so tasty that eating them seems to be more effort than cooking. And a cooked side dish doesn't get any easier than Palong Saag. Spinach, cooked with a blend of Indian spices to melt beautifully in your mouth, is a perfect side to any dish – one I have eaten many times.

INSTRUCTIONS

Get a pan out, put on medium heat, and drizzle with some oil. Add the chopped onion and cook until it's translucent. Add the ginger-garlic paste and green chillies. Mix for a bit and let the spice infuse itself into the onions. Now add the rest of the spices and salt lightly!

Put the heat on high and add your spinach! Cook and salt to your taste and continue cooking until the spinach reduces a lot in size. Add in some cold water (about 500ml) and let this reduce along with the spinach. Drizzle over the lemon juice by squeezing a lemon, and dropping in some fenugreek seeds. Put the lid on and let the dish simmer for 7 minutes.

Now it's up to you how you like the texture, but the longer you cook it, the thicker the consistency!

Beautiful!

A BANGING BHINDI BHAJI FROM BRICK LANE

Serves: **3-4 people**

Prep: **20 minutes**

Cook: **15 minutes**

INGREDIENTS

500g of okra, chopped

½ onion, diced very finely

Oil for cooking

2 tomatoes, diced

Salt and pepper to taste

2 teaspoons cumin seeds

2 teaspoons of minced ginger

Green chillies, diced

1 teaspoon garam masala

1 teaspoon coriander powder

1 teaspoon chilli powder

½ teaspoon turmeric powder

Green/red chillies, for garnish

Bhindi Bhaji is a simple side dish that has accompanied millions of main courses in the UK Indian curry houses. Sure, everyone has their way of making this classic side dish, but with a twist coming from the renowned Brick Lane, this side dish will be just that tad better than the okra you can get from your local curry house.

INSTRUCTIONS

As usual, we'll get our pan hot with some oil. Ensure the pan is over medium heat, and let the oil heat up. Once hot, drop in the onions and cumin seeds. Stir until the onion becomes translucent, and add in the ginger and chillies. Stir for about two more minutes! Let these flavours mix well!

Add the chopped tomatoes and let these cook until they soften (should take about 4 minutes).

Salt and pepper to taste, and add the powdered spices. Stir around until the onions get the tinge of colour from the spices before adding your okra!

Put a lid on it (not as in be quiet, but as in cover the pan!). Let the okra cook until it becomes soft!

Plate, and garnish with coriander!

TIP: When you open the lid, make sure that the collected water under the lid doesn't go into the Bhaji. Otherwise, it becomes slimy.

DAAL

Serves: **3-4 people**

Prep: **25 minutes**

Cook: **20 minutes**

INGREDIENTS

For the lentils:

3 tablespoons vegetable oil

1 onion, finely chopped

1 clove garlic, peeled
and crushed

2 teaspoons ground turmeric

1 teaspoon garam masala

1 teaspoon chilli powder

2 teaspoons all-purpose
seasoning

2 tomatoes, finely chopped

75g moong dal

75g red split lentils

600ml water

For the masala:

4 tablespoons vegetable oil

1 teaspoon cumin seeds

1 dried red chilli

1 teaspoon chilli powder

1 teaspoon asafoetida

4 curry leaves

For the garnish:

Coriander

Green chilli

Daal. The no-bulls**t dish that has fed every kid from the subcontinent since they were a foetus. It's so no bulls**t that if I didn't include it, I'm not sure this cookbook could accurately represent Indian cooking. This Daal is specifically Tarka Daal – a Daal heaving with spices, aroma, and a touch of heat, to be the perfect accompaniment to any main course dish!

INSTRUCTIONS

As you can see from the ingredient list, there are two parts to the dish – the lentils and the masala – but both are simple! Let's start with the lentils. Place a medium saucepan over medium heat and add the vegetable oil. Drop in some onions and let these become translucent! Then add garlic.

Add all your powdered spices and tomatoes as the garlic softens. Mix well, and cook until the tomatoes become very, very soft. Add your lentils into the saucepan, followed by the water. Let the water boil, cover the saucepan and cook the lentils, which will take around 20 minutes. Salt and pepper to taste.

For the masala, it is also very, very simple! Add oil to a pan over medium heat. Add all your ingredients (it's that easy) and stir them in. Then drizzle this masala over your cooked lentils!

CITY SPICE CAULIFLOWER BHAJI

Serves: **3-4 people**

Prep: **15 minutes**

Cook: **15 minutes**

INGREDIENTS

1 medium cauliflower, chopped into small florets

1 tablespoon oil

1 large onion, peeled and finely diced

2 teaspoons ginger-garlic paste

1 teaspoon salt

2 teaspoons of ground cumin

1 teaspoon ground coriander

1 teaspoon of turmeric

½ teaspoon chilli powder

400g tin chopped tomatoes

150ml water

Small bunch of fresh coriander, finely chopped

Take fresh cauliflower delivered daily to City Spice, coat the florets in a beautiful, rich, and luscious tomato sauce with a blend of herbs and spices, and you have a favourite side dish of mine. The whole point of side dishes is that they should be simple and entirely stress-free for the cook. And like all the side dishes I have included, Cauliflower Bhaji stays true to this principle.

INSTRUCTIONS

Get your cauliflower florets and wash them, please! Then pat them dry, or drain them in a colander.

Get a pan and heat some oil over medium heat. Add the onion and ginger-garlic paste, and stir until they soften and the onions become translucent. Salt and pepper to taste, add in your powdered spices, and continue to cook the onions. Pour in tomatoes and the dash of cold water and stir away!

Finally, add your cauliflower and then cook until it reduces, making sure you stir all the flavour into them!

Garnish with coriander. Job done!

ROTIS!

Serves: **3-4 people**

Prep: **35 minutes**

Cook: **7 minutes**

INGREDIENTS

250-300g atta flour

1 teaspoon salt

2 tablespoons oil

1 cup of water

Almost every dish should have this as a side. These healthy round pieces of unleavened bread are the best way to mop up your curry dishes and enjoy them! They can be hard to make, but once you get the hang of it, the feel-good factor for getting these perfect is second to none! Rotis are an essential staple in Indian cooking, so it's important to learn how to cook them perfectly! You need ATTA (a.k.a. chapati flour, which you can find in all your Asian aisles and Asian shops).

INSTRUCTIONS

Take a deep breath before you start, as Roti-making can get sticky. Whisk 250g of atta flour and salt in a large mixing bowl. Add the oil and stir until the flour is clearly grainy and almost like a very powdery substance. Add the water and mix to make a dough that looks unsmooth and dishevelled (I never thought I'd describe a food item as dishevelled, but this is just how it is!)

Knead this dough with your knuckles for ten minutes. Add atta if you need to, but only to make the dough soft, not sticky. Get some oil, drizzle it into your dough, and knead it to get it in. Let this rest for an hour at room temperature so the dough sets.

After an hour, divide the dough into around 6-8 pieces, and roll each piece into a ball (use your Play-Doh skills!), flatten it with your palm to make a disc that you could frisbee, then roll it out into a thin circle, about 7-8 inches in width. Do this for two other pieces, and cook with these first, as it's best to cook as soon as you roll the dough out.

Heat a dry tawa (Google it!) or skillet/pan over medium-high heat. Brush off any flour from the surface of the Roti dough, then place it on the pan. Allow it to cook on the first side until the top of the dough looks dry, then flip it over. You'll have to keep repeating these steps until brown spots develop on the Roti. Try and brush the sides with oil to stop the Roti from sticking to the pan!

Keep repeating until the Roti cooks. If you can, press the dough down with a spatula and watch it puff up. It'll take a few goes to master, but then you will become a Roti legend!

Tip: Prep and store in the freezer so you can cook them when you need to, and it saves time. Also, don't be disheartened if you can't get Rotis perfect the first time! They are hard to make, and it takes a lot of practice! But home-made Rotis are the best!

VEGAN NAAN

INGREDIENTS

120ml warm water

⅔ teaspoon active yeast

⅔ teaspoon organic cane sugar

180g unbleached all-purpose flour

⅔ teaspoon salt

½ teaspoon baking powder

6g garlic, minced

28g plain dairy-free yogurt

20ml olive oil

19g vegan butter

Sea salt

Fresh coriander

I don't think Naan needs any introduction. It is a thick, crunchy, and freshly cooked top-tier bread – lovely to enjoy a curry with. But making a Vegan Naan can be challenging (swapping out the ghee, dairy etc.). Luckily for you, I've done it!

INSTRUCTIONS

Naan is fun to bake! But it requires some skill, so try to take this recipe slowly, as it takes time! First, mix the water, yeast, and sugar in a plastic bowl. Stir quite rapidly and set the plastic bowl aside for 12 minutes to let the yeast take effect. It should soon become frothy and foamy!

Put flour, salt, and baking powder into another large mixing bowl, and whisk quickly to combine these ingredients. Once foaming, add the vegan yogurt bit by bit, stirring it in to ensure the yogurt emulsifies into your mixture. Combine the contents of both bowls (essentially mix the two) and mix with a fork. You should now start to see some dough form which will be sticky.

Now clean and cover your surface with flour and knead the dough into a loose ball; the kneading process should take at most 5 minutes. Place into a bowl, drizzle with oil, cover with a damp towel, and set in a warm place for 2-4 hours.

After waiting for the dough to set, remove it again onto a floured surface and knead for a minute to check the stickiness (add more flour if the dough is too sticky). Divide the dough into 6-8 equal pieces with a knife and knead each piece into a loose ball. Set aside and let them rest for 10 minutes.

Cut either garlic (for a garlic Naan!) or coriander as a garnish for the Naan.

After the dough has had its well-needed rest, roll each piece into an oval shape, like a Naan. Then, drizzle with oil on one side, and stick your garnish onto this wet side.

Take a non-stick pan, heat over medium heat, and once hot, place the Naan wet-side down. Cook for one minute until the edges start colouring, then flip and repeat. You want to keep doing this until the Naan starts to brown, so you can enjoy that lovely charring.

Season with salt to taste, garnish again if necessary, and there you go – Vegan Naan!

PART FIVE:
TITBITS

JUST A FEW MORE THINGS...

ACHA ACHAR PICKLE

INGREDIENTS

8 medium-large limes

2 teaspoons fenugreek seeds

2 teaspoons nigella seeds

1 tablespoon fennel seeds

1 teaspoon chilli powder

1 teaspoon of paprika
or cayenne

1 tablespoon turmeric

¼ to ½ cup salt (you can
always add salt later, but
oversalted pickle is horrible)

1 cup vegetable oil

2 tablespoons mustard seeds

Pickle! Pickle can be used as a condiment, but more importantly, we need it in our cookbook for ever-flavoursome dishes such as Chowle Achar! The recipe below is the perfect homemade pickle. Trust me, it will bring a bit of zing, a bit of spice, and a lot of happiness. However, great things take time! And pickle takes a lot... of time.

INSTRUCTIONS

Get a pan over medium heat and start toasting the dry spices. These include fenugreek seeds, fennel, and nigella seeds, and toast them until a one-of-a-kind fragrance blesses your kitchen! The process will take around 3-5 minutes. Once these spices toast, put them in a blender and grind them into a powder! That's cooking from scratch at its best!

Grab your limes, and place them in a clean, dry glass or ceramic bowl. Add the now grounded spices, paprika or cayenne, turmeric, and salt. Mix well with a clean, dry spoon.

Now bring back the pan and get some oil over high heat! Once the oil is hot, pour it into the bowl with the limes and spices. Mix thoroughly, then transfer to a jar that you can cover.

Now comes the wait. Leave in a sunny place such as a windowsill (let's stick with cloudy for the UK!) and let this pickle... pickle. Leave this out for like 5-7 days, and once it's pickled, stick it in the fridge and let it refrigerate!

VEGAN MINT SAUCE

INGREDIENTS

1 cup vegan yogurt (try and get one that is not extremely bitter)

¼ cup coriander leaves

¼ cup mint leaves

---

1 green chilli

Juice of ½ lemon

¼ teaspoon ground cumin

¼ teaspoon garam masala

¼-½ teaspoon sugar

Salt and pepper to taste

---

2 tablespoons of water

I love this. It makes everything a million times better. A must-have for any vegan starter, a side to any main dish, and even something you can straight up-shot into your mouth. I highly recommend drizzling mint sauce over most starters that you make, coupled with the beauty of mango chutney. Mint sauce is definitely Bonnie (see next recipe!).

INSTRUCTIONS

The sauce is so simple that I promise it is harder to get wrong than it is to get perfect. Grab your coriander leaves, the mint leaves, and the chillies, and blend these until they become very smooth. Once smooth, begin spooning in some yogurt to thicken the blend, and add your dry spices (turmeric for the colour). Whisk everything together until you get a lovely thick sauce. Refrigerate, and use as you wish.

See, easy!

VEGAN MANGO CHUTNEY

INGREDIENTS

400g ripe but firm mango
(these are the best)

1 stick of cinnamon

2 whole cloves

1 teaspoon cumin seeds

1 teaspoon coriander seeds

2 cardamom pods

¾ cup water

1½ teaspoons of ginger-garlic paste

½ cup vinegar

3 whole dried red chillies

1 teaspoon salt

¾ cup brown sugar, or to taste

And Mango Chutney is Clyde! Mango Chutney goes well with everything, so this is perfect to pair with Mint Sauce. We don't mess around with our Mango Chutney; we make it from scratch with beautiful spices and jaw-dropping, ripe, luscious mangoes - a necessity in Indian cooking.

INSTRUCTIONS

Grab your mangoes! Peel them and chop them into one-inch cubes in a saucepan with a tiny bit of oil. Cook the mango over medium heat and add in the dry spices and ginger-garlic paste until it becomes like mush (it's going to be a chutney, after all!). Add vinegar, dried red chillies, and salt and sugar to your taste. Stir continually.

Bring the heat down to its lowest setting and cook for another 20 minutes till the mango resembles a chutney (a very thick sauce). Stir, and then stick in a blender and blend the chutney slightly until it resembles a paste with small mango chunks.

Transfer into a jar and let it cool. Refrigerate, and use as you please!

THE SUPERCALLIFRAGILISTIC EXPIALIDOCIUS VEGAN CURRY BASE

INGREDIENTS

Take a deep breath,
I hope you like onions:

10 large cooking onions – finely sliced

250ml vegetable oil

9 tablespoons garlic-ginger paste (equal amounts of garlic and ginger blended into a paste with a bit of water)

1 carrot, peeled and chopped

¼ head of cabbage, chopped

1 red bell pepper, diced

1 green bell pepper, diced

Water

400ml chopped tomatoes

6 tablespoons of vegetable oil (you need the fatty oil to emulsify the onions!)

1 tablespoon garam masala powder

1 tablespoon cumin powder

1 tablespoon coriander powder

1 tablespoon fenugreek powder

1 tablespoon smoked paprika

1 tablespoon turmeric

You can use a curry base whenever! It's a versatile 'Masala' that you can use to add sauce to your dish, bring some more flavour, and alter the texture of whatever you are making! Curry bases are a standard when cooking professionally (i.e. in restaurants), and I've incorporated some dishes to include a curry base (vegan, of course)! Use my well-perfected vegan curry base recipe to include in many of your curries!

INSTRUCTIONS

Brace yourself, as this is onion heavy! Bring out a large saucepan (the largest in your kitchen) and measure your oil. Let that heat over medium-high heat.

Right! Once the pan is hot, chuck in your onions! Stir consistently for about 20 minutes as we want them to become translucent (the onions make up the main base). Once they are brown, add both peppers, carrot, and cabbage. Combine these as they cook, by stirring them in.

Let this cook away for five minutes (you could watch one of my YouTube videos while you wait!). Pick up your wooden spoon and give the mixture a big stir before adding the ginger-garlic. Then proceed to add your dry spices!

Add your tomatoes, and some water to cover the vegetables. Let this simmer for half an hour before taking it off the heat and then leave to cool.

Now this can get a bit messy. Scoop the mixture into a food processor and blend until it becomes smooth!

Season lightly with salt and pepper, because you will season it when making your curries! Refrigerate and use as and when you wish!

ABOUT THE AUTHOR

Niaz Caan is an award-winning restaurateur and chef renowned for his highly decorated, award-winning curry house, City Spice, in Brick Lane, London.

Born in Whitechapel, Niaz has taken City Spice from strength to strength, with successes in Indian cooking and restaurant service. In 2018, he launched a vegan menu at City Spice. One of the first bespoke vegan menus in an award-winning restaurant, it was lauded by critics and featured on ITV and BBC. Niaz has also been featured on Channel 5 and Channel 4 for his food.

Niaz holds a first-class BSc in Economics from the University of Birmingham. In his spare time, he avidly experiments with new dishes, stays fit, and loves to spend time with his family.

You can find him through the City Spice website: https://www.cityspice.co or bump into him should you visit City Spice, located at 138 Brick Lane, London, E1 6RU.

TESTIMONIALS

"Niaz Caan has taken years of professional cooking experience, made it vegan and made it easy for us readers to follow. I adore what he has done for vegan cooking and, after cooking these tantalising recipes, I wholeheartedly recommend this cookbook. Superb!" – Tommy Miah (MBE), Acclaimed British-Bangla Chef.

"Authentic, creative and most importantly, vegan, the book is inspiring to read just as much as it is to cook with. The recipes are amazing; his innovation in cooking can be clearly seen, and it's no wonder his restaurant is such a big success. Niaz's recipes in this cookbook are a must for any cooking bookshelf. Watch this space!" – Sobur Khan (MBE), President – BBCA Association.